ITALIAN T...

General Editor: Kath...

Petrarch: Select...

The opening lines of the canzone to the Virgin in Petrarch's
own hand (Vat. Lat. 3195)

Petrarch
Selected Poems

Edited with Introduction
Notes and Vocabulary
by

T. Gwynfor Griffith
*Professor of Italian Language and
Literature in the University of
Manchester*
and

P. R. J. Hainsworth
*Fellow of Lady Margaret Hall, Oxford,
and University Lecturer in Italian*

MANCHESTER
UNIVERSITY PRESS

© 1971
Published by
Manchester University Press
Oxford Road, Manchester M13 9PL
ISBN 0 719L 0452 7

Reprinted 1979

Printed by
Unwin Brothers Limited,
The Gresham Press,
Old Woking, Surrey

PREFACE

The purpose of this little volume is very modest: it is to provide the reader who is not familiar with Petrarch's poetry with a brief anthology, and to remove some of the obstacles to appreciation of his work which have troubled some of our pupils in the past.

We have made the selection a comparatively small one; our experience suggests that the reader who really gets to know a few great poems by Petrarch will always return for more, while there is a danger that the student who tries to rush through the lot at first reading may end up with little more than a vague idea that the poet is monotonous. Most of the poems in this book, therefore, have been chosen simply because they are splendid and we like them; but, in addition, a few have been included because they seem to us interestingly to represent a particular kind of writing or to have a certain historical significance for the student of literature.

The notes supply some linguistic and historical information and are intended primarily to assist in the interpretation of difficult passages. Sometimes the aid offered in them takes the form of a translation from the Italian; here our versions are frequently literal, since they are intended, not as a substitute for the original, but as a help in construing it. Where quotations from Latin works have been judged useful in illuminating the text, such quotations are also followed by English versions.

The opinions on Petrarch's work expressed in the introduction have been committed to paper with the student reader in mind: they are intended, not as any kind of final judgement, but as an invitation to discussion. And we should like to add that we are painfully aware that in commenting in the space of a short essay on several aspects of Petrarch's work, as well as on that of several of his predecessors, we have taken dangerous risks; full justice cannot be done to so many so summarily. We believed, however, that it was necessary to try to indicate to the new reader, however imperfectly, what we considered to be the most important features of Petrarch's literary background and of the conventions that affected his writing, and we hope that our observations here, too, will be regarded as an invitation to further investigation. In deciding what needed to be mentioned in so short an introduction, we naturally took into account the help which the English-speaking student already had within easy reach. It should hardly be necessary to state, for instance, that if we have not devoted great space to Dante's lyric poetry, it is not because we underestimate its importance, but because the valuable edition recently published by K. Foster and P. Boyde, to which we refer in our introduction, made it possible for us to devote our meagre space to other matters. Similarly, the appearance of *The Icy Fire* by Leonard Forster enabled us to cut a section on the Petrarchan manner and Petrarch's techniques. We can only trust that what we *have* chosen to write about will seem to the student to be useful in those areas in which he still needs assistance.

We have numbered the poems included in the selection with Arabic numerals 1–60; in all cases the Arabic numeral is followed by a Roman numeral giving the number of the poem in complete editions of the *Canzoniere*.

We wish to express our gratitude to a number of friends and colleagues from whom we have received help. First we must mention the General Editor of this series, Dr. Kathleen Speight, to whose patience and advice we owe a great deal. We also received useful suggestions and criticism from Mr. D. G. Rees, Mr. J. A. Gatt-Rutter and Dr. J. R. Woodhouse, who saw parts of our work in various stages of preparation. Miss J. Salmons and Mr. J. C. Barnes kindly consented to help with the task of reading the proofs, and Mrs. I. J. Roper typed accurately from difficult manuscripts. Finally, we should like to record our appreciation of the kindness and competence of the officials of the Manchester University Press and the printers. None of these, however, is responsible for any opinion expressed.

October 1970   T. G. G.   P. R. J. H.

CONTENTS

INTRODUCTION

I

As we look back on the fluctuations in literary taste between Petrarch's time and ours, it is not too difficult for us to see how past readers have been influenced in their judgements by the intellectual climate of their own age, and to understand why particular historical developments prevented some of them deriving as much pleasure as others had done from reading a poet like Petrarch.[1] It is far harder for us to see ourselves as part of the historical process and to realise that, although unlike each other in our individual tastes and sensibilities, we are all affected in varying degrees by factors peculiar to our time. Of these, the values and prejudices of the national or social group to which we belong, the kind of formal education we have received and the sort of entertainment to which we have been exposed, are only a few of the more obvious. Those of us who have spent some years talking to students of literature about Italian poetry of the fourteenth, fifteenth and sixteenth centuries have become familiar with some at least of the preconceptions which are obstacles in the way of some contemporary readers who wish to understand Petrarch's achievement and importance. These involve both the things he wrote

[1] The student who wishes to study the various kinds of reception accorded to Petrarch in Italy at different periods can begin by reading the brief survey of Petrarchan criticism contributed by E. Bonora to *I classici italiani nella storia della critica*, ed. by W. Binni (Florence, 1960–1), I, 95–167, or that of B. T. Sozzi, *Petrarca* (Palermo, 1963), and following up indications given in their bibliographies. If he is interested in the development of Petrarchism both in Italy and in other countries in Europe, he can begin with Leonard Forster, *The Icy Fire* (Cambridge, 1969), and then turn to the bibliographies appended to C. Calcaterra, 'Il Petrarca e il petrarchismo', in *Questioni e correnti di storia letteraria*, ed. A. Momigliano (Milan, 1949), pp. 167–273. The reader particularly interested in English poetry can begin with the enjoyable essay by D. G. Rees, 'Italian and Italianate poetry' in *Elizabethan Poetry* (Stratford-upon-Avon Studies, 2; London, 1960), pp. 52–69, and then find detailed information in G. Watson, *The English Petrarchans: A Critical Bibliography* (London, 1967).

about and the way in which he fashioned his poems; but it is our experience that initial difficulties are far less frequently to be connected with the former than with the latter.

There are, of course, readers who find Petrarch's situation in the poems odd and his persistence in it exasperating. In many of the novels and films of our time, love is represented by a series of brief encounters not one of which has much lasting significance for the hero (although sometimes an unconvincingly sudden exception is made in the case of the last of the series). To a reader for whom this kind of reading is staple diet, the numberless shifts of mood and variations of feeling conveyed to us in Petrarch's poems about a life-long, unrequited love for Laura are apt to seem remote. Indeed, if the reader combines imprecision of mind with his lack of familiarity with such themes, or if he tends to generalise from his own limited experience, he may describe them as unreal, although they have been real enough to many in the past and are so to some today. The disappointment of this kind of reader, at least, can be largely avoided if we eliminate his preconception that Petrarch's Italian poetry is just the story of a love-affair and that the main pleasure to be expected from it is to be sought in its narrative climaxes; it may be useful, in this connection, if we try in due course to illustrate some of the preoccupations of Petrarch and of other, earlier poets who influenced him.

But those who find in themselves some resistance to reading Petrarch because of his themes seem to be far fewer than those who approach him with the belief that he wrote in a *way* that is likely to repel them. This seems to be at least partly due to the fact that it is one of the penalties of literary education in our schools that the pupil is more likely to have come across the word 'Petrarchism' used as a term of abuse than he is to be familiar with any poems by Petrarch. Moreover, although we have now left some Romantic prejudices behind us, many students still come to the University with one or more of the following assumptions: that the purpose of poetic composition is self-expression (not that Petrarch is disqualified

here), that all poems should be expressions of feeling, that
the more simple and direct such expression of feeling is the
better the poem must be, and that art and artifice are bar-
riers to sincerity (and this perhaps is where the main trouble
lies). Here it must be pointed out that in the past many
kinds of poetry have given pleasure and that in other ages
differing views on the nature of poetry have been held. Some
have thought that the first duty of a poet is to produce a work
of art, a beautiful poem, and not all of these have seen art as
necessarily separate from artifice. For some poets, feeling has
indeed provided an important starting-point, but they have not
for that reason concluded that the process of constructing a
poem should not also make use of ingenuity, wit, intelligence
and even ornament. And over many centuries, mastery of the
resources of language has seemed to countless poets a matter
of supreme importance, leading some even in recent times to
emphasise that poems are written, not with feelings or ideas,
but with words.[2] When Dante wished to pay tribute to the poet
for whom he had more reverence than for any other, he made
a compatriot of that poet's describe him as the man through
whom their language showed what it was capable of ('per
cui / mostrò ciò che potea la lingua nostra').[3] And a French
critic writing of men of letters in the sixteenth century spoke
of 'l'amour quasi-physique du langage' which characterised
the humanists.[4] Perhaps it is this aspect of poetry that brings
us to our greatest difficulty: for the student of Petrarch needs
to know Italian really well to appreciate his full achievement.
Not only must he know Italian well, he must have inherent
delight in the possibilities of language; he must be able to find

[2] 'Un jour, chez Berthe Morisot, se plaignant de la peine que lui
donne le mal de rimer, Degas disait: "Quel métier, j'ai perdu toute
ma journée avec un sacré sonnet sans avancer d'un pas... Et cependant
ce ne sont pas les idées qui me manquent... J'en suis plein... J'en ai
trop".—"Ce n'est point avec des idées qu'on fait des sonnets, Degas,
c'est avec des mots", avait répondu Mallarmé"' (H. Mondor, *Vie
de Mallarmé*, 14th ed., Paris, 1941, p. 684).
[3] *Purgatorio*, vii, 16–17.
[4] Jacques Vier, *Histoire de la littérature française: XVIe–XVIIIe
siècles* (Paris, 1959), p. 12.

pleasure in the marvellous effects which can be produced by
combining sound and sense in Italian. If he is capable of these
things, he will readily enough perceive some at any rate of the
qualities of the poet who wrote:

> che quanto piace al mondo è breve sogno   (I)

or

> La vita fugge e non s'arresta un'ora,
> e la morte vien dietro a gran giornate   (CCLXXII).

But, even if he does have a feeling for lines of this kind, the
contemporary reader may still find the idiom and the manner
of many of Petrarch's poems puzzling, unless he knows something about their literary context. Here again, as in examining
other aspects of Petrarch's work, it is useful to consider the
poetry composed by previous writers in Italy.

II

The lyric tradition which Petrarch inherited from his predecessors and which, for all the innovations he was to make,
determined so many of the characteristics of his own verse,
assumed its essential features, not in Italy, but in Provence
early in the twelfth century. The authors were the troubadours.
The types of verse they wrote were many and varied: political,
religious, moral and war poetry all appear in the anthologies
which have survived; but the type of verse which was most
favoured and which was to have most influence, both within
and outside Provence, was lyrical, and its theme was that
strange phenomenon which came to be termed 'courtly love'.

It was love of a unique kind; almost every aspect of it seems
to have been stylised, even standardised, virtually from the
beginnings of troubadour poetry, and to have been repeated
with only minor variations by poet after poet throughout the
twelfth century and for half the thirteenth. The basic elements
are well known: the lover, that is, the poet, adopts towards his
lady an attitude closely analogous to that of the liegeman vis-
à-vis his lord in feudal society, and uses feudal terminology to

express his subservience and his devotion; he addresses her as 'my lord' (*midons*), he offers his homage and his service, he surrenders to her every right over him; and for himself he can only beg that she show kindness, that she grant him some reward for the service he has rendered her—although the troubadours, when they choose to be explicit, leave no doubt that the reward they desire is the lady's body. This already difficult situation is complicated by the fact that the lady is almost always married, and therefore both lover and beloved must maintain the strictest discretion in order to protect her reputation: the poet can never address her by her real name, but must always use a code name (*senhal*); and every precaution must be taken to avoid arousing the suspicions of the husband, the *gilos* ('jealous one'), as he is usually termed, and also of calumniators (*lauzenjaires*) who might blacken the lady's name by their talk or, worse, report back to the husband. Thus the love-affair, if so it can be called, since the lady more often than not shows no sympathy for her admirer, takes place entirely in an atmosphere of secrecy and suspicion, in which looks, smiles and gestures are the principal means of communication between the lover and the beloved.

Perhaps, as more romantically inclined scholars have been tempted to conclude, such a relationship as it appears in literature reflects the situation in which the poorer and more humbly born troubadours found themselves in life: it is easy, perhaps too easy, to imagine this type of relationship developing between the poet and the wife of his protector and patron, especially when one considers that mediaeval marriages, particularly among the nobility, were normally made, not for love, but for economic and political reasons, and that the woman's say in the matter was minimal. But whether it reflected a real situation or not, courtly love became very early in the twelfth century a convention to which all troubadours, whether of humble or of noble birth (and by no means all the troubadours were of humble birth) submitted themselves, at least in their poetry, whatever they may have done in their lives. No doubt their subjection to the convention was facilitated by the fact that courtly love became not merely a literary but also a social convention.

So far as the poetry of the troubadours is concerned, the courtly love relationship is important less for itself than for the emotional and spiritual consequences which it has. The total dependence of the poet upon his lady and the difficulties he has in establishing even the most elementary contact with her have the effect of turning him in upon himself, of stimulating in him a world of contradictory emotions and aspirations; joy, jealousy, hope, distrust, despair follow each other in rapid succession or may even be experienced at one and the same time. And it is in the experiencing of such emotions in all their intensity that the poet finds an exaltation (*joi*) denied to those who do not love: it is these which he makes the matter of his poetry. In this respect it is far better that the poet should be repulsed by the lady than have his affection returned; for requited love means satisfaction, and satisfaction, once the initial ecstasy has come to its inevitable end, means a quietening of the emotions, whereas repulsion drives the poet back into the inner world of his tensions, with new pains to stimulate and to exalt him. It is of course even better if the lady returns his love and then at a second instance refuses him . . .

But the exaltation of the poet is not, as might seem from what has been said, merely the consequence of a masochistic containment and cultivation of the emotions: it comes also from the conviction that love brings moral as well as emotional stimulation. The loved woman is not merely of perfect physical beauty, as is to be expected, but, by the old Platonic identification of the beautiful and the good, she is also the incarnation of all moral values, in particular of worth (*pretz* or *valensa*) and virtue (*vertutz*), and through contemplating her person or even through thinking of her, the poet stimulates these qualities in himself: he becomes in every way a better man. As one of the best troubadours, Bernard de Ventadour, puts it: Per re non es om tan prezans / com per amor e per domnei, / que d'aqui mou deportz e chans / e tot can a proez' abau. / Nuls om ses amor re no vau. ("Through nothing does a man win as much worth as through love and the cult of woman: from this comes my pleasure and my song, and everything conducive to prowess. No man is of value without love.')[5]

In so far as the twentieth century thinks of love at all, it tends to consider it a personal experience, which may contain certain constant factors, but which is, to a large extent, limited and defined by circumstances and by the characters of the individuals involved. For the troubadours almost the opposite was the case; love was an experience fundamentally identical for all those who experienced it. Consequently, since it was the unchanging and universal essence of the love experience which they wished to express, they excluded from their verse, as far as they could, the personal and individual elements that the contemporary reader has been accustomed by novels and verse of his own time to expect: the drive was towards abstraction of language and thought, and also towards repetition. Hence the notorious monotony of troubadour verse: again and again the poets protest in very similar terms their devotion to the lady and to love, their repentance if they have given offence, their longing to reveal their love and yet their fear to do so, the trembling and sickness which overcomes them at the sight, or even at the thought, of the beloved, the folly and yet sublimity of their condition, and so on. And the lady herself becomes a pale, generic figure, with blonde hair and a beautiful body, who is alternately kind and cruel to the poet, and, whether kind or cruel, is always his inspiration.

Since the motifs of the love-experience and the language in which they were expressed tended to so great a degree of abstraction and stylisation, it was possible for a rigorous and virtuoso technique of versification to be developed, and, although verse-forms also tended to follow certain set patterns, it was largely in this field that the troubadours attempted to prove themselves as poets. In particular, they attempted to show mastery of the *canso* (Italian *canzone*), the lyric form par excellence. The *canso* was usually between forty and eighty lines

[5] Bernard de Ventadour, *Chansons d'Amour*, ed. Moshé Lazar (Paris, 1966), No. 11.

long, and divided into a number of stanzas each of equal length, with normally a short *codetta* in which the poet addressed either his song or the minstrel (*joglar*) who was to sing it. In the *canso* the rhymes were all-important, and the poet showed his skill by his ability to manipulate difficult, yet appropriate and harmonious, rhyme-schemes. One of the favourite schemes, for example, was the *canso unissonans*, in which the rhymes of the first stanza were repeated in the same order throughout the remaining stanzas of the poem, an achievement not to be underrated, since each stanza was normally of eight or more lines in length and in itself contained three or four pairs of rhymes. With Arnaut Daniel (who was writing roughly from 1180 to 1210), the cult of the virtuoso rhyme reached its peak: as a suitable correlative to his allusive and punning style (the *trobar clus* as it was called), Daniel developed the most complicated rhyme structures, cultivating especially the device known as *rims equivocs*, whereby words of identical sound but of different meaning were rhymed together. The results were admired by Petrarch and Dante, but have won only tepid applause from modern critics, with the exception of Ezra Pound.[6]

Provençal poetry was known and appreciated in cultural circles outside Provence from about the middle of the twelfth century, and the troubadours themselves frequently spent long periods abroad. The natural consequence was that in Northern France, England, Spain, Germany and Italy, the Provençal mode of writing was sooner or later adopted into the vernacular, with lesser or greater modifications depending on the country. In Italy the process was somewhat circuitous: in the north, possibly because there was a larger influx of troubadours than elsewhere, very probably because of the similarities between Northern Italian dialects and Provençal, a number of Italians imitated the troubadours, not in their own language, but in Provençal itself, and the fashion persisted until well into the

[6] Ezra Pound, 'Arnaut Daniel', in *Literary Essays of Ezra Pound*, edited and with an introduction by T. S. Eliot (London, 1954), pp. 109–48.

second half of the thirteenth century. But none of them, not even the famous Sordello, whom Dante meets in his ascent of Purgatory (*Purg*. VI), did more than repeat what their models had already done, and their influence on the later lyric in Italy was negligible.

It was in Southern Italy and Sicily that the Italian love-lyric found its true cradle. There courtly verse was written in an ennobled vernacular[7] during the reign of the Emperor Frederick II (d. 1250). This Hohenstaufen ruler of the former Norman kingdom was the centre of the most brilliant, luxurious and intellectual court in contemporary Europe. He himself and two of his sons, as well as officials and courtiers associated with them, were among the poets of the so-called 'Sicilian' school. Whether occasional fresh, realistic elements in the poems of some Sicilians should be attributed to a heritage of earlier, autochthonous popular poetry now lost or to French influences brought to bear during the Norman period, has been the subject of controversy; what is certain is that the vast majority of the poems of the Sicilians owe much in matter and manner to the troubadours.

The intention of the Sicilians was doubtless to realise in their own vernacular the modes of feeling and expression of the courtly lyric as they had been formulated in Provence and imitated with some minor innovations in France and Germany: they seemed less concerned with finding a new direction than with heightening some of the features to be found in their Provençal predecessors. Consequently we find rehearsed in their poetry the whole spectrum of attitudes to love, to the beloved and to the business of writing outlined above à propos of the Provençal poets: the poet puts himself in the same position of subservience and dependence, adores and complains in the same way, suffers the same pain and exaltation: and he writes in a similar abstract and stylised language, giving to Italian words the technical meaning that their Provençal

[7] The poems of the Sicilians have, with one or two exceptions, come down to us in Tuscanised versions. Most scholars now accept the thesis that they were originally composed in a refined form of Sicilian.

equivalents had held in the lyric, and importing into Italian, with the necesssary phonetic adaptations, terms that existed in that language but had no equivalent in his own.

What innovations there are in the verse of the Sicilians fall into the category of shifts of emphasis rather than that of genuine novelties; yet these shifts of emphasis are of some consequence for later Italian verse. Already in the Sicilians, elements that are not central to the experience of being in love tend to be excluded: not only do all the poems which we have, with the exception of one or two sonnets, treat exclusively of love, where the Provençal poets had tended to vary their subject-matter, but within those love-poems there is a concentration of attention on the emotional conflicts of the poet which tends to exclude external factors: the jealous husband and the calumniators of Provençal poetry fade into the background, and similarly the end of the poet's desires becomes, generally speaking, far less explicitly sexual than it had been in troubadour verse. In accordance with this greater internalisation of the love-experience, there is a tendency to reflect more upon the nature of that experience, and, especially in the sonnet, to attempt to define it, although such philosophising never passes beyond commonplace considerations of whether love should be termed an accident or a substance, and of how love is born in the heart through the medium of the eyes. Yet, slight though they are, it is from such changes of emphasis that the *dolce stil novo* will be born.

In matters of versification the Sicilians were, in comparison with their Provençal models, conservative: they made no attempt to imitate the virtuoso displays of Arnaut Daniel, and were restrained even in the use they made of such devices as the *canso unissonans*, mentioned above. At the same time their achievement and skill were considerable: they established the two forms that were to dominate Italian lyric poetry, the sonnet and the canzone, and showed an ability to manage both forms efficiently. The sonnet was, so far as we know, invented by them, probably, as tradition has it, by Giacomo da Lentini, one of the oldest members of the school and perhaps the most

important. The canzone, imitated from the Provençal *canso*
with perhaps some influence from the German *Minnesang*, has
already in Sicilian verse the tripartite stanzaic structure that is
familiar in later poets, and there is too that other common
feature of later verse, the tendency to give to each *canzone* an
individual metrical structure instead of following set patterns
in the Provençal manner.

If moderate in metre, in respect of word-play and puns the
Sicilians attempted on occasion to show a proficiency equal to
that of the later Provençal poets. Giacomo da Lentini, for
example, bases a whole sonnet on the root *viso*, the first line
of which runs:

> Eo viso e son diviso da lo viso[8]

i.e. 'I see, and am separated from, her face'. And in the middle
of a canzone Pier della Vigna produces the monstrous alliteration and puns of:

> La morte m'este amara, ché l'amore
> mutòmi in amarore.[9]

i.e. 'Death is bitter to me, since it changed my love to bitterness'. Such games with words give to the verse of the Sicilians
as to their models that firework effect which is often attributed
to Petrarch and his imitators, but which was, in fact, part of
the tradition they inherited.

The importance of the Sicilians is historical rather than
aesthetic: for although occasional poems evince a certain charm
and freshness, the greater part of their verse is repetitive and
impersonal. Of the thirty or so poets to whom our manuscripts
ascribe poems (and only in the case of Giacomo da Lentini
have we a considerable body of work) only one or two show any
individuality of theme or technique, and even in these cases
the originality is of the slightest: a fresh image, a new paradox,
and little more. Giacomo da Lentini, Rinaldo d'Aquino,
Stefano Protonotaro, Pier della Vigna, Giacomino Pugliese,

[8] *La poesia lirica del Duecento*, a cura di C. Salinari (Turin, 1968),
p. 98.
[9] *Poeti del Duecento*, a cura di G. Contini (Milan–Naples, 1960),
Vol. 1, p. 126.

Guido delle Colonne and the rest remain largely names to
which we can attach the poems we have.

Frederick II died in 1250. After some disturbances, he was
succeeded as ruler of Sicily and Southern Italy by his illegitimate son, Manfred, and under Manfred the school of Sicilian
poetry continued to prosper, although, so far as we can tell,
without any change or innovation occurring. But in 1266 Manfred's forces were defeated by the French at the battle of
Benevento, and he himself was killed. His death meant the end
of Swabian power in Southern Italy, and the great administra-
tive machinery and the splendid court which Manfred had
inherited from his father were destroyed. With that destruction
came the end of the Sicilian school proper (although versifiers
were to continue to imitate its manner until the end of the
century) and also the end of Southern Italy as a centre for
literary activity. Primacy now passed to the independent cities
of Central Italy, and in that new environment, with its bourgeois and commercial tendencies, the lyric tradition underwent
considerable modification.

The first necessity was to expand upon the thematic and
linguistic base which the Sicilians had provided, and the poet
who answered the need, although not in a manner that was to
content his successors, was Guittone d'Arezzo (c. 1230–94),
the first Italian poet by whom we have a large body of verse
(50 canzoni and some 250 sonnets) and the first to assume a
distinct literary personality. Guittone sensed the inadequacy of
the Sicilians' narrow and conventional vocabulary, and pursued
in his own verse a policy of linguistic expansion and experi-
ment, drawing indiscriminately, though energetically, on all
the sources open to him; Latin, French, Provençal and the
dialect of his native Arezzo all provided words and forms with
which to swell and enrich the poetic language. With the wider
possibilities given to him by his new linguistic freedom, Guittone was able to indulge in experiments in technique denied to
the Sicilians; he made attempts to rival in Italian the *trobar
clus* of Arnaut Daniel, and experimented on his own account
with complicated canzone structures and with variations on the

sonnet form. The results may not be pleasing, but they represent a necessary broadening of scope, an expansion of poetic language in order to handle concepts and theoretical discussion.

Equally significant is the direction in which the content of Guittone's verse points; in contrast to the Sicilians, Guittone moves towards greater psychological and social realism. Biographical and circumstantial details appear, if only spasmodically, in his verse, and metaphors taken from the world of commerce are used to describe the pain and exaltation of love. On a more general level, some parts of Guittone's work show an acceptance on the part of the lover of a certain autonomy and individuality in the woman; and, as a consequence of this, the attitude of the lover changes; as well as asking for favours, he at times asserts himself and demands a response, and, as well as praising, on occasion he condemns his lady's conduct in strong uncomplimentary language.

The honest bourgeois element in Guittone eventually forced him to come to terms with a factor which the Sicilians had conveniently ignored, although its significance had been felt by Cappellanus in his treatise *De Amore* and by some of the later troubadours. Guittone saw that however much the poets might protest that love, if folly, was an ennobling and beneficent folly, its basis lay in adultery and carnality, and that consequently it could be nothing but sinful. The outcome of this gradual realisation was that sometime in his mid-thirties Guittone abandoned love-poetry altogether, and turned his attention exclusively to moral, religious and political themes, thereby effecting a further expansion in the scope of the Italian lyric, and one that was to bear fruit in the doctrinal verse of Dante both within the *Comedy* and outside it, and in the political poems of Petrarch.

Guittone had his imitators: but it is clear that he was also symptomatic, if not the actual cause, of a crisis in the development of the Italian lyric. First and foremost, there was the language problem; an aesthetic criterion, so obviously lacking in Guittone's verse, had to be found in order to regulate the poetic language, to decide what forms and what words were in fact acceptable, and then to assimilate them into a coherent whole. Intimately connected with this problem was the problem of love itself; what was in fact the nature of this strange and contradictory passion, what were its effects, and, above all, was it, as Guittone and others had affirmed, a destructive folly? And, assuming that it was not folly, how could it be taken seriously in an environment different from that of the courts in which it had first flourished and with which so many of the traditional attitudes as expressed in the lyric were connected? Already in Tuscany the so-called *poeti giocosi* were beginning to write sonnets in which the courtly relationship and aspirations of the lover were parodied in no uncertain terms.

Neither problem was susceptible of a definitive solution: obviously any solution that was reached had to depend very much on the nature of the individual poet. But from Guittone onwards, serious lyric poetry in Italy evinces a concern, even an obsession, with the problems of language and love. Guinizzelli, Cavalcanti and Dante will all compose more or less explicitly doctrinal poetry on the nature of love: Dante will devote the first book of his treatise *De vulgari eloquentia* to considerations on the nature of an appropriate poetic language; and on a more general level it is fair to say that whatever triumphs were achieved by the three poets mentioned above were the result of the reassessment of the bases of the lyric forced upon them by Guittone and his disciples. The same is true of Petrarch; it is his success in solving the linguistic problem and his detailed exploration of so many facets of love that constitute two of the principal reasons for his greatness as a poet.

But before Petrarch, developments occurred which he could not but take into account. The poets responsible for them are generally considered as a group and referred to as the poets of the *dolce stil novo* or *stilnovisti*, on the basis of a passage in *Purgatorio* (XXIV, 49–62) in which Dante draws a distinction between the 'sweet new style' and the style of preceding poets. It is not at all clear from this passage, or from other passages in Dante, which poets he holds to have developed the 'sweet new style', but in recent Italian literary criticism the *stilnovisti* are generally considered to be seven in number. Three of them, Lapo Gianni, Gianni Alfani, and Dino Frescobaldi, are minor poets on any reckoning; it is the four remaining poets who are of interest and importance for the development of the tradition: they are the Bolognese Guido Guinizzelli (c. 1230–76), the Florentines Guido Cavalcanti (c. 1255–1300) and Dante Alighieri (1265–1321), and Cino da Pistoia (c. 1270–1336).

The eldest of the four, Guido Guinizzelli, is something of a transitional figure. At least two of the sonnets in his slender *canzoniere* (seven canzoni and fifteen sonnets) are in the manner of the *poeti giocosi*, and other poems, presumably the earliest, are in the Guittonian idiom. But in certain of Guinizzelli's poems there are indications of an attempt to solve the dilemmas outlined above. Instead of following up the Guittonian movement towards realism, Guinizzelli moves in the opposite direction, that is, towards greater abstraction. He abandons once and for all the social circumstances surrounding the central love-experience, such as the calumniators, the husband, and the conventional incidents of a love-affair. The woman herself who had begun in Guittone's verse to take shape as an individual, or at least as a force to be reckoned with, returns to the background to become again an ideal figure. And the full force of the poet's attention falls upon the emotional conflicts within himself, upon praise of the beloved, and upon reflections on the nature of love. In this way, Guinizzelli eliminates from his poetry elements which could only be fictitious and irrelevant in the bourgeois society of Central Italy, and re-asserts the validity of the central experience. At the same time this step is saved from being retrogressive by the cultivation of a new style which avoids the worn clichés of the Sicilians and the troubadours no less than the irregularity of Guittone. The prevailing characteristic of this style is, as Dante indicates in his address to Guinizzelli in Purgatory (XXVI, 112), *dolcezza*, a word which in this context has none of the cloying associations of the English 'sweetness', and should perhaps be translated by 'harmoniousness', were that not such an unharmonious word. To be more specific, Guinizzelli excludes altogether the more outrageous foreign or dialectal elements of Guittone, and makes no attempt at technical flamboyance; instead he blends in a melodic equilibrium forms carefully selected from the Sicilians, from Guittone and from his own Bolognese dialect. At the same time the traditional vocabulary of the lyric is severely curtailed, and curtailed in such a way as to give a certain emphasis to key terms such as *beltà*, *valore*, *gentile*, *vertute*, *umiltà*, which are seen to contain the essence of the love-experience. By isolating them from the mass of courtly vocabulary, and supporting them with melodious unemphatic phrases and a series of delicate images taken from light and nature, Guinizzelli achieves verse which is both more precise and more evocative than that of any of his predecessors.

The natural tendency of such verse is upwards out of the world: and it is with Guinizzelli that the aethereal element always implicit and occasionally explicit in courtly verse comes to the fore. Although the physical beauty of the lady continues to be praised, greater emphasis is now placed on certain moral qualities which she possesses and which have an uplifting effect on the poet, as we can see in the following lines:

> Passa per vìa adorna, e sí gentile
> ch'abassa orgoglio a cui dona salute,
> e fa 'l de nostra fé se non la crede;
>
> e no·lle pò apressare om che sia vile;
> ancor ve dirò c'ha maggior vertute:
> null'om pò mal pensar fin che la vede.[10]

The association of the beloved and love with virtue leads in Guinizzelli's most famous poem (*Al cor gentil rempaira sempre amore*)[11] not only to the identification of the noble heart and love, but also to the justification of love before God: at the end of the poem Guinizzelli has no hesitation in affirming that his beloved is like an angel and that he was not wrong to love her. The affirmation had been made before by Guittone and by

[10] *Idem*, Vol. II, p. 472.
[11] *Idem*, Vol. II, p. 460.

some of the later troubadours, but it is only here that there is full consciousness of its implications, for of course it answers, perhaps in the only possible way, accusations against the immorality and destructiveness of love.

Cavalcanti follows in the direction which Guinizzelli's later verse had indicated: melody, evocativeness, abstraction are the keynotes of his verse. Writing in a language which is basically purified Florentine, Cavalcanti puts even more restrictions on the imagery and vocabulary of the lyric than his predecessor. The luminous and natural images are attenuated still further, as are the physical features of the beloved, and the verse rests entirely on the melodic and evocative use of a small number of abstract or generic words, as in the following sonnet, in which an attempt is made to express the ineffable:

> Chi è questa che vèn, ch'ogn'om la mira,
> che fa tremar di chiaritate l'âre
> e mena seco Amor, sí che parlare
> null' omo pote, ma ciascun sospira?
>
> O Deo, che sembra quando li occhi gira,
> dical' Amor, ch'i' nol savria contare:
> cotanto d'umiltà donna mi pare,
> ch'ogn'altra ver' di lei i' la chiam'ira.
>
> Non si poria contar la sua piagenza,
> ch'a le' s'inchin' ogni gentil vertute,
> e la beltate per sua dea la mostra.
>
> Non fu sí alta già la mente nostra
> e non si pose 'n noi tanta salute,
> che propiamente n'aviàn canoscenza.[12]

But there is novelty: not only is Cavalcanti, in spite of the suggestive quality of his verse, still more precise than Guinizzelli, in that the key words of his lyric take on the air almost of a technical terminology, but he develops in some depth a technique of analysing the emotions which had previously been used only sporadically. Instead of simply contrasting two or more conflicting desires or sensations, he allows

[12] *Idem*, Vol. II, p. 495.

his heart, mind, thoughts, eyes and the agents which he calls *spiriti* to assume a certain independence, and to struggle or debate with each other, as if they were individuals in conflict within him. Although such analysis never becomes more than schematic, it confers upon his verse a new psychological subtlety and dramatic intensity, and it will in its turn provide a starting-point for the more refined analysis undertaken by Petrarch.

There is too a different attitude towards love: whilst Cavalcanti still associates love with the noble heart, he sees the consequences of love as suffering and the death of the intelligence, perhaps even of the soul, as he indicates in his most famous and most difficult poem, the doctrinal canzone *Donna me prega*.[13] His other poems bear out his conclusions there; almost all are pessimistic analyses of pain, in which the key words are *pianto, sospiri, pena, morte*. In view of his pessimism, Cavalcanti, whilst preserving a chastity of desire (in that he wishes no more of his beloved than to contemplate her and to receive her greeting) cannot, as Guinizzelli had done, attempt to make love into a morally justifiable passion, and is driven into a solitary and negative heterodoxy.

With Dante we come to the poet who, even if we discount the *Divine Comedy* (itself essentially a development from the lyric tradition), is the most complex and original writer of verse before Petrarch, and, in view of the variety of styles and attitudes which his lyric verse displays, the most difficult to characterise succinctly, the one constant factor in his development seeming to be a determination to explore to the full the technical and expressive possibilities of each mode that he adopts.

After a period of uninspired but perhaps necessary imitation, first of conventional Tuscan versifiers writing in the Sicilian manner, and then of Cavalcanti, Dante made his first, and, so far as the lyric tradition is concerned, most important, step forward with the *Vita Nuova*, the collection of verse with a prose commentary which he put together probably in 1292 and

[13] *Idem*, Vol. II, p. 522.

1293. The *Vita Nuova* represents the only example before Petrarch's *Rime* of a large group of poems artistically ordered in a narrative sequence. So far as we can tell, earlier Italian poets had made little attempt to organise their *canzonieri*: their concern had remained the individual poem, not the poem as part of a larger whole. In the *Vita Nuova*, on the other hand, the poems and the prose commentary 'tell a story', however ideal and distorted that story may be, and the relevance of each poem is affected by its position in the story. More significantly, the *Vita Nuova* introduces a new concept of love: the earlier chapters of the book contain examples of Dante's early imitative verse, but from Chapter XIX onwards Dante includes verse which is clearly inspired by Guinizzelli but which goes far beyond his concept of the *donna angelicata*. The association of the beloved with the divine here becomes explicit; the full stress of the verse, and of the commentary, falls on the fact that her virtues, which are very much the virtues of the Cavalcantian and Guinizzellian *donna*, are of a more than human origin, and that she is a representative on earth of the divinity in heaven:

> Ella si va, sentendosi laudare,
> benignamente d'umiltà vestuta;
> e par che sia una cosa venuta
> da cielo in terra a miracol mostrare.[14]

At the same time Dante abandons one of the corner-stones of the traditional love-ethic, the desire for a response from the beloved. Already attenuated in Cavalcanti and in his own earlier verse into a desire for a look or a greeting, this desire is now transformed into a readiness to be content with meditating on the beloved and praising her. Since in this way the last residues of the physical and earthly elements in the love-experience are dispersed, the experience becomes not merely justifiable, as it had been for Guinizzelli, but praiseworthy and rationally advisable. By meditating on the angel in human

---

[14] *Dante's Lyric Poetry*, ed. K. Foster and P. Boyde (Oxford, 1967), I, 78. The student is strongly urged to read this collection of poems and the introduction to it.

form, the lover improves himself as a Christian. Through the
creature he is led to the Creator. Hence the religious aura of the
Vita Nuova as a whole, hence too the essence of the *Comedy*,
in which Beatrice leads Dante through various stages of illu-
mination to the godhead. Thus the exaltation traditional in the
love-experience reaches the mystical heights to which it had
always tended.

This protraction of the love-experience to its spiritual conclusion is Dante's principal contribution to the tradition. In
the verse which follows the *Vita Nuova*, Dante explores fields
which are of importance as stages in his own development but
which otherwise in the history of the lyric are something of a
dead end. From love poëtry he turns his attention to allegorical
and doctrinal verse: and although he is able, thanks to the
device of allegory, which permits him to present concepts in
the guise of female figures, to retain much of the vocabulary
and many of the attitudes of the love-poet, he to a large extent
abandons *dolcezza* as a criterion for poetry, sometimes in
favour of a deliberate harshness, and in any case going beyond
the limits which he and other poets had previously imposed
upon the vocabulary and imagery of their verse; in particular,
he introduces into verse a terminology and modes of procedure
taken from scholastic philosophy, a process already begun by
Guinizzelli and Cavalcanti in one or two poems, but now
rigorously extended and explored by Dante. There is, however, one group of four poems by him which will have a
definite influence on Petrarch: these are the *rime petrose*.
Here, in imagery drawn from the seasons and the countryside,
Dante expresses a sensual, savage dependence on a woman
who is ruthless towards him (*di pietra*); the verse reflects this
harshness and, at the same time, becomes the means for a display of technical virtuosity in which Dante shows himself
superior, not merely to the despised Guittone, but to the
masters of the *trobar clus*, introducing into Italian and dominat-
ing the difficult *sestina* form invented by Arnaut Daniel, and
even composing a double *sestina*. Although Petrarch will be
largely unaffected by the sensuality of the *petrose*, he will on

occasion imitate their technical bravura and their harshness, and, more important, he will develop the nature imagery that Dante here introduces into the lyric.

But the *dolce stil* was not dead: it was in fact to flourish well into Petrarch's lifetime and even beyond. It has, however, only one other practitioner of note, Cino da Pistoia. Cino provides a link between Dante and Petrarch: he exchanged sonnets with the former and he received on his death the tribute of a sonnet (XCII) from the latter. The connection was not merely conventional: for in Cino some of the attitudes and motifs that will be fully developed by Petrarch receive their first expression. To a large extent he rehearses themes and styles found in Cavalcanti and Dante, with particular stress on the pain of love in the manner of the former, and with the harmoniousness of style that had characterised the verse of both. But there is a difference: although Cino uses the old terminology, it loses in his verse that clarity of definition, that air of being a technical vocabulary which it had had in the two earlier poets. When, for example, he praises the angelic qualities of his beloved, his praise takes on the air of a compliment rather than being a true appreciation of the transcendental in her. This loss gives to his poetry a certain indecisiveness of tone which frequently results in a weary plaintiveness very different from the exact pain of Cavalcanti. As a natural consequence of this blurring of the absolute, there are indications of a return towards the world: incident and changes of heart play a much greater part in Cino's verse than in that of the other poets of the *dolce stil*, and the lady begins to assume, as well as spiritual attributes, certain physical features, which, however schematic and ideal, are of this earth.

In this way Cino sets the stage for Petrarch. Petrarch will develop the conflict implicit in Cino's verse between the longed-for (but uncertain) transcendental and the demands of the earthly, with the inevitable consequence that the traditional absolute schemata will be broken up in a personal emotional spectrum. Thereby the lyric will be liberated from the old constrictions: in a word, it will be humanised.

III

In what he entitled his *Rerum vulgarium fragmenta*, which have become known also by the Italian labels of *Canzoniere* and *Rime sparse*, Petrarch left us 317 sonnets, 29 canzoni, 9 sestine, 7 ballate and 4 madrigali. These and the *Trionfi* were not the only verse he wrote in Italian: he was the author, too, of a number of short poems which he did not see fit to include in his final collection of *Rime*. In Italian prose, only one short letter of his has come down to us; in Latin, on the other hand, he left a vast amount of prose as well as verse. It was on his voluminous Latin works that his reputation among his contemporaries was principally based, and it was through those works that he was to exercise so great an influence on the development of humanism in Italy. To the lyric poems he wrote in Italian he referred as *nugellae*, but although they were in some ways obviously less weighty than his Latin writings, it is difficult to believe that Petrarch was unaware of the importance of the sonnets and canzoni to whose composition, revision and arrangement he devoted so much care over a period of more than forty years. He wrote in one of them that, had he known that his Italian poems were to find favour, he would have given more care to both their quality and quantity:

> S'io avesse pensato che sí care
> fossin le voci de' sospir miei in rima,
> fatte l'avrei, dal sospirar mio prima,
> in numero piú spesse, in stil piú rare. (CCXCIII)

But he alleged that, now that Laura was dead, he had no longer the same capacity in composition, while, when she was alive, he had written only in order to relieve his heart of some of its pain:

> E certo ogni mio studio in quel tempo era
> pur di sfogare il doloroso core
> in qualche modo, non d'acquistar fama;
> pianger cercai, non già del pianto onore. (CCXCIII)

We may treat both statements with a little scepticism, for the poems written after the death of Laura show no loss of ability (but, if anything, a gain), while his revision and treatment of his earlier poems are hardly such that we should assume that their purpose was exclusively therapeutic (any more than we should conclude that his letters were written only for the individuals to whom they were originally addressed, when they were just as clearly intended for the admiration of posterity).

Although some of the poems in the *Rime* are on political and religious themes, the vast majority are concerned with emotions and reflections connected with Petrarch's love for Laura. In his letter *Posteritati*, he tells us little about this aspect of his life (and it is at least arguable that the single sentence he there devotes to it is not altogether consistent with what he wrote elsewhere):

Amore acerrimo sed unico et honesto in adolescentia laboravi, et diutius laborassem, nisi iam tepescentem ignem mors acerba sed utilis extinxisset.

(In my youth I laboured under love of a most fierce kind, but single and honest, and I should have done so for much longer, had not death, bitter, but useful, extinguished the fire which was already beginning to die down.)

On the fly-leaf of his copy of Virgil he wrote rather more informatively:

Laurea, propriis uirtutibus illustris et meis longum celebrata carminibus, primum oculis meis apparuit sub primum adolescentie mee tempus, anno Domini m⁰ iij^c xxvij die vj⁰ mensis Aprilis in ecclesia sancte Clare Auin. hora matutina; et in eadem ciuitate eodem mense Aprili eodem die sexto eadem hora prima, anno autem m⁰ iij^c xlviij⁰ ab hac luce lux illa subtracta est, cum ego forte tunc Verone essem, heu! fati mei nescius. Rumor autem infelix per literas Ludouici mei me Parme repperit, anno eodem mense Maio di xix⁰ mane. Corpus illud castissimum atque pulcerrimum in loco Fratrum Minorum repositum est, ipso die mortis ad uesperam. Animam quidem eius, ut de Africano ait Seneca, in celum, unde erat, rediisse persuadeo michi. Hec autem ad acerbam rei memoriam amara quadam dulcedine scribere uisum est, hoc potissimum loco qui sepe sub oculis meis redit, ut scilicet nichil esse debere quod amplius mihi placeat in hac uita et, effracto maiori laqueo, tempus esse de Babilone fugiendi crebra horum inspectione ac fugacissime etatis estimatione conmonear, quod, preuia Dei gratia, facile erit preteriti temporis curas superuacuas spes inanes et inexpectatos exitus acriter ac uiriliter cogitanti.

(Laura, illustrious through her own virtues, and long famed through my verses, first appeared to my eyes in my youth, in the year of our Lord 1327, on the sixth day of April, in the church of St. Clare in Avignon, at matins; and in the same city, also on the sixth day of April, at the same first hour, but in the year 1348, the light of her life was withdrawn from this light of ours, while I, as it chanced, was in Verona, unaware of my fate. The sad news reached me in Parma, in the same year, on the morning of the 19th day of May, in a letter from my Ludovicus. Her chaste and lovely form was laid to rest at vesper time, on the same day on which she died, in the burial place of the Brothers Minor. I am persuaded that her soul returned to the heaven from which it came, as Seneca says of Africanus. I have thought to write this, in bitter memory, yet with a certain bitter sweetness, here in this place that is often before my eyes, so that I may be admonished, by the sight of these words and by the consideration of the swift flight of time, that there is nothing in this life in which I should find pleasure, and that it is time, now that the strongest tie is broken, to flee from Babylon; and this, by the prevenient grace of God, should be easy for me, if I meditate fiercely and manfully on the futile cares, the empty hopes, and the unforeseen events of my past years.)

There is no documentary evidence to connect Laura with any real woman, although attempts to identify her have been made by ingenious biographers (notably de Sade, who sought to prove that she was probably the wife of a member of his family, Hugues de Sade, and the daughter of Audibert de Noves). Because we do not know about her, some critics have suggested that she did not exist. Indeed, this argument started while she was still alive, for in 1336 Petrarch wrote in a letter to his friend, Giacomo Colonna, the following sentences:

'Quid ergo ais? finxisse me michi speciosum Lauree nomen, ut esset et de qua ego loquerer et propter quam de me multi loquerentur; re autem vera in animo meo Lauream nichil esse, nisi illam forte poeticam, ad quam aspirare me longum et indefessum studium testatur; de hac autem spirante Laurea cuius forma captus videor, manufacta esse omnia, ficta carmina, simulata suspiria. In hoc uno vere utinam iocareris; simulatio esset utinam et non furor! Sed, crede michi, nemo sine magno labore diu simulat; laborare autem gratis, ut insanus videaris, insania summa est. Adde quod egritudinem gestibus imitari bene valentes possumus, verum pallorem simulare non possumus. Tibi pallor, tibi labor meus notus est; itaque magis vereor ne tua illa festivitate socratica, quam yroniam vocant, quo in genere nec Socrati quidem cedis, morbo meo insultes.'

('What then do you say? That I have invented the lovely name of "Laura" in order to have someone to talk about, and in order to set people talking about me, but that, in truth, I have no "Laura" in mind, except that poetical laurel to which I have aspired, as my long and untiring study bears witness; and as to this breathing "laurel", with whose beauty I seem to be captivated, all that is made up—the songs feigned, the sighs pretended. On this point would that your jests were true! Would that it were a pretence, and not a madness! But, believe me, it takes much trouble to keep up a pretence for long; while to labour pointlessly in order to appear mad would be the height of madness. Add that, though in our actions we can feign sickness when we are well, we cannot feign actual pallor. You know well both my pallor and my weariness; and so I fear you are making sport of my sickness by that Socratic form of humour called "irony", in which Socrates must yield the palm to you.')

There seems to be no reason to doubt Petrarch's word, but there seems to be no reason either to expect the Laura of the poems to be identical with the Laura of life.[15] Why should we expect Petrarch to provide us with an objective account of the external circumstances of his relations with one actual person, rather than with a work of imagination in which he has drawn upon his experience, his reading, his meditations and his day-dreams? Was Dante insincere if the Beatrice he imagined in *Purgatorio* and *Paradiso* was different from what the daughter of Folco Portinari had been on earth? If Petrarch relived his emotions in his imagination (and reflected upon them) as he

[15] This is not the place for an evaluation of the vast literature concerned with Laura. The student will find a sound and enjoyable beginning in E. Carrara, 'La leggenda di Laura' in that author's *Studi petrarcheschi* (Turin, 1959), pp. 77–111. For details of many other works on the subject, sound and unsound, he can consult C. Calcaterra, *op. cit.*

made poems, then we should expect that process itself to transform them. (It has often been observed that Laura is portrayed as more compassionate as well as more concrete in the poems written after her death than in those composed during her life.) Was that not part of the purpose?

Perché, cantando, il duol si disacerba. (XXIII)

There is little enough about Laura in the *Rime*; there is much more about Petrarch. But even if there had been more about her, and if it could be shown that the Laura of poetry had become different in various details from the real person or persons who contributed to the poet's conception of her, that would invalidate neither Petrarch's image of her nor the power of his verse. In other words, if the non-existence of the 'real' Laura had somehow been proved, it would make no difference to our view of Petrarch's poems.

If the reader comes to Petrarch with the idea that his poems are just the story of a love-affair, he may find them very different from what he has imagined. While it is not true, as is sometimes stated, that his passion has no history, that it is static (for it is, in fact, constantly shifting), it is true that the essential external events are so few that they have already been summarised in the brief passages from Petrarch that we have quoted. But to lead the reader to expect merely the narrative of a love-affair would be a misleading form of introduction to the content of the *Rime*. What is *not* misleading, as an introduction, is the poem which Petrarch himself placed first in the collection: for this leads the reader to expect that he will be told, not only about love, but also about the vanity of Petrarch's hopes and grief; that he will be made to feel the invincible melancholy of a man who has lived with the conviction that the things which bring him such hopes and such despair, such joy and such misery, which determine his moods and his actions, are things which he should never have allowed to continue in such dominion over him. In connection with this fundamental theme, the *Secretum* is an invaluable commentary to the *Rime*. In it Petrarch has to admit the existence of elements that he himself considers unworthy, both in his desire for fame (which was so strong a motive in his literary career) and in his love for Laura. And he also has to admit that, even when he is intellectually convinced of the unworthiness of the objects of his cares, his will is quite unable to master his feelings about them. The *Rime* include beautiful love-poems of various kinds; but they also include poems that will speak to any man who has found himself absurdly pleased or wretchedly dejected by matters which his convictions and his reason insist are not worth the candle, and who has realised that such absorption in the unworthy is a betrayal of what is worthy:

> e veggio 'l meglio et al peggior m' appiglio. (CCLXIV)

That is a situation which can be understood and felt by a reader whose idea of a love-affair is very different from Petrarch's, even if he has not yet come to Petrarch's final conclusion:

> che quanto piace al mondo è breve sogno. (I)

If we read the appropriate passages in the *Secretum*, we find that Petrarch, in discussing his relationship with Laura, claims that he had 'not loved her body more than her soul'. ('Hanc presentem in testimonium evoco, conscientiamque meam facio contestem, me (quod iam superius dixeram) illius non magis corpus amasse quam animam.') Under close questioning, however, he is forced to admit that under the compulsion of love and youth he had desired what St. Augustine refers to in the dialogue as something base ('Turpe igitur aliquid interdum voluisti'). Laura, however, had proved inflexible and unyielding. No flattery or entreaty had been able to undermine her chastity and, in time, Petrarch, who had earlier been grieved by her resolution, had come to accept it and be grateful for it. This situation is reflected in the *Rime*: Laura is an ideal creature, firm and virtuous, throughout; Petrarch goes through innumerable moods and attitudes. The *Rime* are mainly about his states of mind and some of his convictions tested in relation to the consistently virtuous Laura.

Just as he does not tell us much about the nature of Laura
in the *Secretum*, so he tells little also in the *Rime*. His descriptions of her physical appearance do not comprise the kind of
particulars which would allow an acquaintance to identify her;
but they are written about in such a way as to leave us in no
doubt about their overwhelming effect on the poet, as one sees
for example in a poem which describes her weeping (even
though in it Petrarch is making use of terminology that was
already conventional in the love-lyric and was to become even
more so in the work of his successors):

> La testa or fino, e calda neve il volto,
> ebeno i cigli, e gli occhi eran due stelle,
> onde amor l'arco non tendeva in fallo;
>
> perle, e rose vermiglie, ove l'accolto
> dolor formava ardenti voci e belle;
> fiamma i sospir, le lagrime cristallo. (CLVII)

More powerful still is a poem which tells of the conversion of
her beauty into dust:

> Gli occhi di ch'io parlai sí caldamente,
> e le braccia e le mani e i piedi e 'l viso,
> che m'avean sí da me stesso diviso
> e fatto singular da l'altra gente;
>
> le crespe chiome d'or puro lucente
> e 'l lampeggiar de l'angelico riso,
> che solean fare in terra un paradiso,
> poca polvere son che nulla sente. (CCXCII)

Her moral and intellectual qualities, as he describes them, are
those of a perfect creature:

> In nobil sangue vita umile e queta
> et in alto intelletto un puro core,
> frutto senile in sul giovenil fiore
> e 'n aspetto pensoso anima lieta,
>
> raccolto ha 'n questa donna il suo pianeta,
> anzi 'l Re de le stelle, e 'l vero onore,
> le degne lode, e 'l gran pregio, e 'l valore,
> ch'è da stancar ogni divin poeta.

> Amor s'è in lei con onestate aggiunto,
> con beltà naturale abito adorno,
> et un atto che parla con silenzio,
>
> e non so che nelli occhi, che 'n un punto
> po far chiara la notte, oscuro il giorno,
> e 'l mel amaro, et addolcir l'assenzio. (CCXV)

Since her qualities are so consistent, the reader becomes preoccupied, not with her, but with the frequent contradictions and variations in Petrarch's attitude to her. There are times when he treats her as if she were a descendant of some of the ladies described by the poets of the *dolce stil novo*, bringing out the good in her poet and leading him to heaven:

> Gentil mia donna, i' veggio
> nel mover de' vostr' occhi un dolce lume,
> che mi mostra la via ch'al ciel conduce;
> e per lungo costume
> dentro là dove sol con amor seggio,
> quasi visibilmente il cor traluce.
> Questa è la vista ch'a ben far m'induce,... (LXXII)

Or again:

> da lei ti ven l'amoroso pensero,
> che mentre 'l segui, al sommo ben t'invia,
> poco prezzando quel ch'ogni uom desia,... (XIII)

But sometimes he speaks of her as if she were a reflection of the *douza ennemia* of some Provençal poets, a creature whose rejection of Petrarch is merely the result of her pride:

> Mille fiate, o dolce mia guerrera,
> per aver co' begli occhi vostri pace
> v'aggio proferto il cor, m'a voi non piace
> mirar sí basso colla mente altera. (XXI)

Yet in his old age, he is prepared to accept that this rejection

was really for the sake of his own salvation, and he thanks her
for preserving their virtue:

> Or comincio a svegliarmi, e veggio ch'ella
> per lo migliore al mio desir contese,
> e quelle voglie giovenili accese
> temprò con una vista dolce e fella;
>
> lei ne ringrazio e 'l suo alto consiglio,
> che, col bel viso e co' soavi sdegni,
> fecemi, ardendo, pensar mia salute. (CCLXXXIX)

This view of himself, as a man whose desires needed to be
thwarted for the sake of a higher good, fits in, not with those
poems which present a picture of a spiritual love, but with an
early admission of physical desire:

> Con lei foss'io da che si parte il sole
> e non ci vedess' altri che le stelle,
> sol una notte, e mai non fosse l'alba! (XXII)

There are times when his rejected love causes him such despair
that he declares that, if he could be sure that death would
relieve him of his passion, he would kill himself:

> S'io credesse per morte essere scarco
> del pensiero amoroso che m'atterra,
> colle mie mani avrei già posto in terra
> queste membra noiose e quello incarco. (XXXVI)

It is in this state of obsession that he is driven to walk in
deserted places, intolerant of human companionship, as he
tells us in the magnificent sonnet beginning:

> Solo e pensoso i piú deserti campi
> vo mesurando a passi tardi e lenti,
> e gli occhi porto per fuggire intenti
> ove vestigio uman l'arena stampi. (XXXV)

In such moods he is apt to think of the harm caused by his
love:

Io son de l'aspettar omai sí vinto
e de la lunga guerra de' sospiri,
ch'i' aggio in odio la speme e i desiri
et ogni laccio onde 'l mio cor è avinto.

Ma 'l bel viso leggiadro, che depinto
porto nel petto e veggio ove ch'io miri,
mi sforza, onde ne' primi empi martiri
pur son contra mia voglia risospinto.

Allor errai quando l'antica strada
di libertà mi fu precisa e tolta,
ché mal si segue ciò ch'agli occhi agrada;

allor corse al suo mal libera e sciolta,
ora a posta d'altrui conven che vada
l'anima che peccò sol una volta. (XCVI)

But there are other moods. There are times when he blesses
the day when it all began:

Benedetto sia 'l giorno e 'l mese e l'anno
e la stagione e 'l tempo e l'ora e 'l punto
e 'l bel paese e 'l loco ov'io fui giunto
da' duo begli occhi che legato m'hanno;

e benedetto il primo dolce affanno
ch'i' ebbi ad esser con amor congiunto,
e l'arco e le saette ond'i' fui punto,
e le piaghe che 'nfin al cor mi vanno.

Benedette le voci tante ch'io
chiamando il nome de mia donna ho sparte,
e i sospiri e le lagrime e 'l desio;

e benedette sian tutte le carte
ov'io fama l'acquisto, e 'l pensier mio,
ch'è sol di lei, sí ch'altra non v'ha parte. (LXI)

There are occasions when he dares to hope that Laura will yet
be kind to him and when he admits that he would not exchange
his bitter-sweet life for another:

A ciascun passo nasce un penser novo
de la mia donna, che sovente in gioco

> gira 'l tormento ch'i' porto per lei;
> et a pena vorrei
> cangiar questo mio viver dolce amaro,
> ch'i' dico: «Forse ancor ti serva amore
> ad un tempo migliore;
> forse a te stesso vile, altrui se' caro». (CXXIX)

And there are moments when he will even more significantly admit that he enjoys his passion, with the sighs and tears it brings him:

> Pasco 'l cor di sospir, ch'altro non chiede,
> e di lagrime vivo, a pianger nato;
> né di ciò duolmi perché in tale stato
> è dolce il pianto piú ch'altri non crede. (CXXX)

and unequivocally:

> Lagrimar sempre è 'l mio sommo diletto. (CCXXVI)

After all, everything else in the world is transient:

> ahi, nulla altro che pianto al mondo dura! (CCCXXIII)

Moreover, the root of his bitterness is so sweet that no state is superior to his:

> viva o mora o languisca, un piú gentile
> stato del mio non è sotto la luna:
> sí dolce è del mio amaro la radice. (CCXXIX)

These contradictory emotions are overshadowed by the conviction that all his vacillations in feeling, the delirium and the joy, the despair in which he occasionally wallows and the hopes on which he sometimes precariously builds, are all vanity, and that a man of firm religious faith should be concerned with worthier things:

> Io son sí stanco sotto 'l fascio antico
> de le mie colpe e de l'usanza ria,
> ch'i' temo forte di mancar tra via
> e di cader in man del mio nemico. (LXXXI)

In that sonnet his love for Laura is presented, not as a way to
heaven, but as a passion that may cause him to fall into the
hands of the devil. Elsewhere, he states that he is weary of this
battle and sees no prospect of relief:

> Non spero del mio affanno aver mai posa. (CXCV)

He feels that the way to heaven lies by another path, and that
it is high time he turned to it:

> ora la vita breve e 'l loco e 'l tempo
> mostranmi altro sentier di gire al cielo
> e di far frutto, non pur fior e frondi.
>
> Altr'amor, altre frondi et altro lume,
> altro salir al ciel per altri poggi
> cerco, che n'è ben tempo, et altri rami. (CXLII)

Once again, Laura is clearly presented, not as an angelic
creature, not as a ladder to heaven, but as human and a diver-
sion from the Christian life. And so one could go on, if one
had space enough, illustrating many other aspects of the lover's
experience as conveyed by Petrarch (as, for example, in the
imaginary meetings with Laura, virtuous still, but kinder to
her poet and curiously more human and real, that he writes of
after her death). But to quote but a few of Petrarch's poems is
sufficient to show that he was aware, as few have been, of the
contradictory aspects of love and of its conflicts, both within
itself and with other forces.

It is this awareness of conflict and of oppositions, allied to
his notable taste for concentrated expression and rhetorical
balance, that presumably underlies his liking for a rhetorical
device which some of his readers have disliked and many of his
imitators battened upon: antithesis. At its worst, it can be just
playing with words. But we come to realise, as we cherish some
of Petrarch's phrases in the memory, not only that it can be a
very appropriate way of expressing his inner contradictions,
but that it frequently seems a way of resolving them, an attempt
to put them together in a precise and balanced relation to one

another, to know them, and to transcend them by creating
something beautiful out of combining them with apposite
words: the harmony of the poems of the *Rime*. Appropriately
used, antithesis is a device that permits the author forcefully
to render, at one swift stroke, the seemingly contradictory
elements in the situation he wants to convey, as in

> ... con un volto
> che *temer* e *sperar* mi farà sempre. (CXIX)

To describe or analyse this picture (in which we have both the
lover's hope that his lady will be kind and, at the same time,
the awe and respect that hold him in perpetual fear of destroy-
ing their relationship) would be to dilute the poetry, and
Petrarch, not being Guittone, does not do so. Similarly, he
suggests the mortal and immortal elements in Laura with the
greatest economy, and without any use of abstract adjectives,
in the line:

> lei che 'l *ciel* ne mostrò, *terra* n'asconde. (CCLXXIX)

And when he extends his use of this device to include a series
of antitheses, he can rapidly sketch a very adequate picture of
the ingredients of a lover's uncertainty:

> Se 'n solitaria piaggia, rivo o fonte,
> se 'nfra duo poggi siede ombrosa valle,
> ivi s'acqueta l'alma sbigottita;
> e come amor l'envita,
> or ride or piange, or teme or s'assecura;
> e 'l volto che lei segue ov' ella il mena
> si turba e rasserena,
> et in un esser picciol tempo dura;
> onde a la vista uom di tal vita esperto
> diria: «Questo arde, e di suo stato è incerto». (CXXIX)

The balance of the *Canzoniere* is surely to be found not so
much in the ingenious patterns which some critics have sought
in the order of its poems as in the equilibrium of these conflicting elements in Petrarch's presentation of his experience,

in the perfection of his final arrangements of them within individual poems.

Antithesis is only one of the many rhetorical devices that Petrarch used. Another which allowed him to concentrate a great deal in a single line was asyndetic enumeration. This does not appeal equally to all readers. The extreme example

> fior frondi erbe ombre antri onde aure soavi (CCCIII)

was admired by Bembo,[16] but Trissino thought that it sounded like German.[17] Yet another example of a concentrating device is the use of parallel pairs like

> *pentito* e *tristo* de' miei sí spesi anni (CCCLXIV)

or

> fuggir *la carne* travagliata e *l'ossa* (CXXVI),

where Petrarch is using, not synonyms, but words that, while carrying different meanings and overtones, powerfully reinforce one another. Similar strengthening of effect can also be achieved, not by adding to the load of meaning, but, as in Welsh systems of *cynghanedd*, by repetition of certain vowel sounds or by consonantal alliteration, as in

> come quella che *ferro* o *vento sterpe* (CCCXVIII)

or

> e rotto 'l *nodo*, e 'l *foco* ha spento e sparso (CCLXXI)

We have no space to illustrate the many facets of Petrarch's virtuosity; they have been the subject of many studies.[18] But

[16] *Prose e rime*, ed. Dionisotti (Turin, 1960), pp. 168 and 172.

[17] *Opere* (Verona, 1729), II, 23.

[18] For a valuable introduction to 'the Petrarchan manner', the student should read Leonard Forster, *The Icy Fire* (Cambridge, 1969), esp. pp. 1–60. For Petrarch's techniques, see E. Bigi, 'Alcuni aspetti dello stile del canzoniere petrarchesco' in his *Dal Petrarca al Leopardi* (Milan–Naples, 1954, pp. 1–14); D. Alonso, 'La poesia del Petrarca e il petrarchismo (mondo estetico della pluralità)', in *Studi petrarcheschi,*

we should note that the devices he uses frequently help his
lines to establish a firm hold on our memories, just as in Welsh
poetry lines in *cynghanedd* almost invariably get a better grip
on us than those in the free metres. It is true that such poetry
is harder to digest on first hearing than a simpler, more facile,
apparently more spontaneous type of verse. It is true, too, that
in the case of Petrarch the fact that memory and meditation
upon it are so important a part of the poetic process combines
with the application of learning and rhetorical skills to deprive
some of his poems of any illusion of immediacy. His is an art
which presents to us something that has lain long in the
imagination, gaining in associations, reflections, and overtones
—a poetry that is the 'foster-child of silence and slow time'.
All art is necessarily mediate, not immediate; Petrarch's more
so than most.

To that kind of art Petrarch was inclined by his reflective
nature and by his learning. On his experience of life he
meditated with the knowledge of a man who had immersed
himself enthusiastically in Latin literature. It was natural,
therefore, that he should enrich his compositions with parallels
and analogies from classical mythology and ancient history,
ranging from numerous borrowings from Ovid's *Metamorphoses* (as in XXIII) to brief mention of Hannibal's private
life in Apulia (CCCLX)—a borrowing from the elder Pliny.
There was nothing forced about this, any more than in his
habit of writing on his manuscript of the *Rime* comments in
Latin addressed to himself and concerned with their future
revision: for Latin language and literature were part of his
daily life. It was only to be expected, therefore, that he should
enrich Italian by adapting to it statements, images or idioms
which he had found in the classics and which were relevant to

VII (1961), 73–120; M. Fubini, 'Il Petrarca artefice' in *Studi sulla
letteratura del Rinascimento* (Florence, 1947), pp. 1–12; and U. Bosco,
'Il linguaggio lirico del Petrarca tra Dante e il Bembo' in *Studi
petrarcheschi*, VII, 121–32. But, above all, the student should read
Bembo's *Prose*; his appreciation of what Petrarch could do with words
has never been equalled.

his purpose, like his adaptation of Ovid's

> Video meliora, proboque,
> Deteriora sequor (*Met.*, VII, 20–1)

to give in Italian the line

> e veggio 'l meglio et al peggior m'appiglio. (CCLXIV)

Many more such examples will be indicated in our notes to individual poems, for in the field of the lyric Petrarch made greater use than did previous poets of elements adapted from classical literature. Such elements undoubtedly constitute an important factor in the wealth of his images and the dignity of his poetic idiom.

Nor was his learning confined to Latin authors.[19] Those very techniques which we mentioned as being among the typical features of his writing suggest that he had learnt much from the Provençal poets, who were so fond of assonance, internal rhymes, alliteration and antithesis (although it must be remembered that he could have derived such features indirectly, through the work of earlier Italian poets, as well as directly). As for previous Italian literature, we have already noted occasions on which Petrarch conceived of his love for Laura in the terms used by poets of the *dolce stil novo*. Indeed, Petrarch himself indicates his interest in both Provençal and early Italian poetry in canzone LXX, where each stanza ends with a line borrowed from a previous poet: one from a Provençal poem (probably written by Arnaut Daniel), the others from Guido Cavalcanti, Dante Alighieri, Cino da Pistoia and

---

[19] On the subject of Petrarch's reading, his knowledge of classical and modern authors and the nature of his humanism, the bibliography is vast: see the appropriate section in Calcaterra, *op. cit.* We think the student should still begin with the fundamental work by P. de Nolhac, *Pétrarque et l'humanisme* (Paris, 1907), 2 vols. But he should then turn to G. Billanovich, 'Il Petrarca e i classici' in *Studi petrarcheschi*, VII, 21–34, and follow the directions indicated in it and the same author's *Petrarca letterato: lo scrittoio del Petrarca*, Rome, 1947. He will find details of recent works on the subject (by Billanovich and others) in the bibliography appended to A. E. Quaglio, *Francesco Petrarca* (Milan, 1967), esp. pp. 232–6. In English, he should read J. H. Whitfield, *Petrarch and the Renascence*, Oxford, 1943.

an earlier canzone by Petrarch himself (a poet whom, by
virtue of his constant revision of his poems, he studied profoundly, a fact which no doubt contributed greatly to his con-
sistency of language and style).

These influences from earlier literature were certainly not
limited to matters of form or technique. The ways in which
previous poets treated love helped to mould Petrarch's conception of his love for Laura. And certainly his reading of Cicero,
St. Augustine and the Bible are reflected in the moral sense
with which Petrarch reflects upon his condition and which is
one of the striking features of the *Rime*, from the sonnet introducing the collection to the final canzone to the Virgin. It is
this moral sense and the melancholy reflections arising from it
that bind to the love poems of the *Rime* the poems of patriotic,
religious and political inspiration which the poet chose to
include in the same collection, like the sonnets on the corrup-
tion of the papal court at Avignon and the great patriotic
canzoni *Italia mia* and *Spirto gentil*. These poems display the
same sadness in the poet's contemplation of public affairs as
do his love-poems in the consideration of his private affairs.
Italia mia and *Spirto gentil* also show the same sense of the
vanity and transience of all that belongs to the world of men.
That is why Attilio Momigliano was so rightly drawn to conclude that

La poesia patriottica del Petrarca nasce da uno stato d'animo
simile a quello della poesia amorosa e da un atteggiamento della
fantasia uguale a quello della poesia amorosa: perciò essa, almeno
nelle due canzoni maggiori, fa tanta impressione sul lettore.[20]

But all Petrarch's self-knowledge, all his moral sense, all
his study of Latin literature and of Provençal and Italian lyric
poetry, would have been of little avail, if he had not been so
great a master of language, if he had not had the ear to allow
him to make from disparate elements a language consistent
with itself, and with his constant search for dignity and

[20] 'L'elegia politica del Petrarca' in his *Introduzione ai poeti* (Florence,
1946), p. 9.

elegance.[21] Petrarch's language has great range, from the nimble

> Aura che quelle chiome bionde e crespe
> cercondi e movi, e se' mossa da loro
> soavemente, e spargi quel dolce oro
> e poi 'l raccogli e 'n bei nodi il rincrespe (CCXXVII)

to the nobly ponderous echoes of scripture in

> Io son sí stanco, sotto 'l fascio antico
> de le mie colpe e de l'usanza ria,
> ch'i' temo forte di mancar tra via
> e di cader in man del mio nemico.
>
> Ben venne a dilivrarmi un grande amico,
> per somma et ineffabil cortesia;
> poi volò fuor de la veduta mia,
> sí ch'a mirarlo indarno m'affatico.
>
> Ma la sua voce ancor qua giú rimbomba:
> «O voi che travagliate, ecco 'l camino;
> venite a me, se 'l passo altri non serra».
>
> Qual grazia, qual amore o qual destino
> mi darà penne in guisa di colomba,
> ch'i' mi riposi e levimi da terra? (LXXXI)

(surely one of the most moving statements we have of the spiritual weariness of man under the persistent weight of oppression by his own nature). But, however various, his style never loses dignity, syntactical balance, elegance, harmony. Its qualities were appreciated in the sixteenth century by Pietro Bembo:

Ma come che sia, venendo al fatto, dico che egli si potrebbe considerare, quanto alcuna composizione meriti loda o non meriti, ancora per questa via: che perciò che due parti sono

---

[21] There is no room here for a discussion of Petrarch's language. The student should read 'Preliminari sulla lingua del Petrarca' in Petrarca: *Il Canzoniere*, ed. G. Contini, 6th edition (Turin, 1975). For a view of Petrarch in the linguistic context of his time, he can consult the relevant pages of G. Devoto, *Profilo di storia linguistica italiana* (Florence, 1964), and B. Migliorini–T. Gwynfor Griffith, *The Italian Language* (London, 1966).

quelle che fanno bella ogni scrittura, la gravità e la piacevolezza;

quelle che fanno bella ogni scrittura, la gravità e la piacevolezza; e le cose poi, che empiono e compiono queste due parti, son tre, il suono, il numero, la variazione, dico che di queste tre cose aver si dee risguardo partitamente, ciascuna delle quali all'una e all'altra giova delle due primiere che io dissi. E affine che voi meglio queste due medesime parti conosciate, come e quanto sono differenti tra loro, sotto la gravità ripongo l'onestà, la dignità, la maestà, la magnificenza, la grandezza, e le loro somiglianti; sotto la piacevolezza ristringo la grazia, la soavità, la vaghezza, la dolcezza, gli scherzi, i giuochi, e se altro è di questa maniera. Perciò che egli può molto bene alcuna composizione essere piacevole e non grave, e allo 'ncontro alcuna altra potrà grave essere, senza piacevolezza; sí come aviene delle composizioni di messer Cino e di Dante, ché tra quelle di Dante molte son gravi, senza piacevolezza, e tra quelle di messer Cino molte sono piacevoli, senza gravità. Non dico già tuttavolta, che in quelle medesime che io gravi chiamo, non vi sia qualche voce ancora piacevole, e in quelle che dico essere piacevoli, alcun' altra non se ne legga scritta gravemente, ma dico per la gran parte. Sí come se io dicessi eziandio che in alcune parti delle composizioni loro né gravità né piacevolezza vi si vede alcuna, direi ciò avenire per lo piú, e non perché in quelle medesime parti niuna voce o grave o piacevole non si leggesse. Dove il Petrarca l'una e l'altra di queste parti empié maravigliosamente, in maniera che scegliere non si può, in quale delle due egli fosse maggior maestro.[22]

Bembo's attachment to Petrarch was of great importance, not only in determining the direction of sixteenth-century Petrarchism, but also in the subsequent history of the language and literature of Italy. At a time when Italian writers were concerned with raising their vernacular to the status of a great literary language comparable with Latin and Greek, Bembo offered them a solution to their problems of language and style. As a latinist, he had been among those classical scholars most opposed to electicism: he had urged those who wanted to achieve

[22] *Prose*, II, ix, in *Prose e rime*, ed. Dionisotti (Turin, 1960), pp. 146–7. If he wishes to see Petrarchism and Bembism in proper historical perspective and understand their significance in the history of Italian literature, the student should not miss C. Dionisotti's introduction to this edition of Bembo. For interesting observations on the service rendered by Petrarchism to other literatures, he should read Leonard Forster, *The Icy Fire*, esp. pp. 61–83 ('European Petrarchism as training in poetic diction').

a good style in Latin not to put together elements borrowed from different authors and different periods, but to write prose like Cicero and verse like Virgil. The programme he offered Italian authors was a similar doctrine of imitation applied to the vernacular: Italians who wished to write well should write with the style of Boccaccio and of Petrarch ('con lo stile del Boccaccio e del Petrarca')—prose like Boccaccio's, verse like Petrarch's. This process of vying with the authors of the greatest age in Florentine literature and of building a literary language based on their fourteenth-century Florentine, offered a practical solution to men who lived in various parts of the Italian peninsula and whose native dialects differed greatly from one another. To point to a literary language which could be acquired, like Latin or other dead languages, by the study of the illustrious writers of the past, made unity in the literary language possible in a country which had no political capital and a multitude of spoken tongues.

For this purpose, Petrarch was a superb model. Although his language was capable of considerable variety, it was nevertheless consistent in usage and tone and both dignified and reasonably restricted in diction. If you are seeking something imitable, it is no use going to an author whose range covers all registers and whose vocabulary offers infinite variety; that would only leave you with the problem of seeking elsewhere for guidance in your choice of what to accept. Petrarch also suited Bembo's very literary and bookish tastes, for it was part of Bembo's doctrine that the language of literature should not approach the spoken language except when that could be done without loss of gravity ('La lingua delle scritture...non dee a quella del popolo accostarsi, se non in quanto, accostandovisi, non perde gravità'). He was deeply concerned about purity of diction, advocating the use of 'le piú pure, le piú monde, le piú chiare...le piú belle voci'. It is not surprising, therefore, that he had reservations about Dante, who used words that were uncouth or otherwise unsuitable ('...ora le non usate e rozze, ora le immonde e brutte, ora le durissime usando, e allo 'ncontro le pure e gentili alcuna volta mutando e guastando...').

And to him as to other writers of the sixteenth century, who
were so concerned with raising their literary language to a new
dignity by exploitation of the literary lessons that humanism
had given them and the linguistic elements that their classical
education had placed at their disposal, Petrarch was bound to
be of special interest; he had had the taste to use Latin to
ennoble his Florentine without doing violence to the linguistic
base (as happened in the works of some fifteenth-century
writers). His works were neither in popular Florentine nor in
offensively latinate Italian. Professor Dionisotti makes a very
just comment on this matter in his introduction to Bembo:

Al di là del Petrarca e del Boccaccio, era, secondo il
Bembo, la decadenza. Anche qui non si può dire che avesse
torto. L'equilibrio di due lingue nell'opera del Petrarca era
stato eccezionale: in Boccaccio già si vede come l'educazione
umanistica o premesse troppo sul volgare o addirittura ten-
desse a escluderlo. L'alterno processo durò per tutto il Quattrocento...

Italy did not achieve political unity until the second half of
the nineteenth century; it is only now in the twentieth that that
unity, combined with growth in education and great changes in
communication, is bringing about a substantial degree of
linguistic unity. For centuries, therefore, Italy presented the
interesting spectacle of a literature in Italian largely written by
authors who did not speak the language they wrote. For a
great many of them the way to eminence in Italian literature
was along the path indicated by Bembo: study of a literary
language based on fourteenth-century Florentine and of its
greatest authors. In this linguistic situation, literary tradition
was bound to become a matter of paramount importance, and
in the field of Italian lyric poetry no author was to have greater
influence than Petrarch, the model Bembo himself had
favoured. It is hardly necessary to add that in the sixteenth
century other nations than Italy conceived the ambition of
possessing a great literature and a great literary language; to
them Italy became a model, her literature a third classical
literature to plunder. And to them, too, Petrarch was a figure

of interest, not only because of the aid Petrarchism afforded to all those who sought a new poetic diction, but also on account of the intrinsic interest of the Petrarchist treatment of the traditions of courtly love. If we read Du Bellay, Surrey, Garcilaso, we have before us but a few of the scores of examples of Petrarch's influence outside Italy. And if, within the bounds of Italian literature, we read poets as different as Della Casa, Leopardi and Ungaretti,[23] each of them will remind us that, in every century between his own life and ours, Petrarch has seemed to other writers using the Italian language to be a poet worthy of the most serious consideration and of the most careful stylistic study.

[23] Recent manifestations of Petrarchism and their background are the subject of the inaugural lecture of Frederic J. Jones, *The development of Petrarchism and the modern Italian lyric* (Cardiff, 1969).

A SUMMARY OF THE PRINCIPAL EVENTS
IN PETRARCH'S LIFE

1302   Petrarch's father, a notary, Ser Pietro Petracco by name, is banished from Florence by the Blacks and takes refuge with his wife in Arezzo.

1304 July 20th Petrarch is born at Arezzo.

1305–11   Petrarch's mother lives with her son at Incisa in the Valdarno, the home of the Petracco family.

1307   Gherardo, Petrarch's brother, is born.

1311   The family move to Pisa.

1312   They move on to Provence, where there is both greater security and better scope for Ser Petracco's talents, in view of the fact that the seat of the Papacy is now Avignon.
               Ser Petracco establishes his family at Carpentras, about fifteen miles to the north-east of Avignon.

1312–16   Petrarch receives a basic grounding in grammar and rhetoric from the Tuscan schoolmaster Convenevole da Prato.

1316–20   •He studies civil law at the University of Montpellier.

1318 or 1319   Death of Petrarch's mother: this occasions a Latin elegy, the earliest poem of Petrarch's to have survived.

1320–26   He continues his legal studies at Bologna, with some interruptions.

1326   Death of Ser Petracco: Petrarch willingly abandons law and returns to live a somewhat frivolous life at Avignon.

1327 April 6th   He sees Laura in the Church of St. Clare at Avignon.

1330   Financial difficulties lead Petrarch to enter the Church: although committed to celibacy and to the tonsure, he never undertakes more than nominal pastoral duties.
                 He becomes a protégé of the powerful Colonna family, and is appointed household chaplain to Cardinal Giovanni Colonna.

1333   He visits Paris and returns to Provence via Ghent, Liège (where he discovers the oration of Cicero *Pro Archia*), Aix-la-Chapelle, and Cologne.

1336–7   He makes a six-month visit to Rome, where he is the guest of Bishop Giacomo Colonna. The first surviving selection that Petrarch made of his verse in Italian dates from this period.

1337   He purchases a villa at Vaucluse, the 'closed valley', at the head of which is the source of the River Sorgue: from now until his definitive departure for Italy in 1353 he will spend as much time as possible there, composing, thinking, and enjoying the solitude and simplicity of the countryside.

1337   The birth of Petrarch's illegitimate son, Giovanni, at Avignon.

1338 or 1339   He begins at Vaucluse the composition of a series of biographies of illustrious Romans entitled *De viris illustribus*.

He also starts work on his Latin epic, the *Africa*, based on the exploits of Scipio Africanus.

About this time he begins to call himself 'Petrarca', presumably because it was a more euphonious and also more latinate name than 'Petracchi', the form he had hitherto used.

He writes the first of his 'triumphs', the *Triumphus Cupidinis*, as well as further sonnets and canzoni in Italian.

1341   In the previous year the University of Paris and the Roman Senate had both offered Petrarch the poet laureate's crown: he had accepted the offer of the latter. He now travels to Naples in the company of Azzo da Correggio, the future tyrant of Parma. In Naples he successfully undergoes an examination by his sponsor for the laureateship, King Robert, of his knowledge of literature and philosophy. After a month, he goes on to Rome. On April 8th he receives the crown on the Capitoline Hill. In Petrarch's estimation it was his greatest public triumph.

He passes most of the remainder of the year at Parma, now in the hands of Azzo da Correggio and his brothers; he completes a draft of the *Africa*.

1342   He returns to Avignon: there he makes the first of his several unsuccessful attempts to learn Greek, and drafts the first form of the *Canzoniere* (some 100 poems).

1343 He makes friends at Avignon with Cola di Rienzo, the man who will try to break the tyranny of the warring noble families of Rome and substitute a constitution modelled on that of the ancient city.
Gherardo becomes a Carthusian monk.
Francesca, Petrarch's daughter, is born.
He writes the *Secretum*, an analysis in dialogue form of his spiritual inadequacies, and begins his *Rerum memorandarum libri*, a treatise on the cardinal virtues.
In September he visits Naples again, principally on a diplomatic mission for the Pope, Clement VI, and for Cardinal Colonna: from there he travels to Parma.

1344 He buys a house in Parma, and takes up residence there. He continues the *Rerum memorandarum libri*, but abandons the work altogether after completing only four books: he also writes several more Italian poems, including the *Triumphus Pudicitie*, and, probably, *I' vo pensando* (CCLXIV). Towards the end of the year Parma is besieged by the Mantuans and the Milanese: see the note to *Italia mia* (CXXVIII), no. 21 in this selection.

1345 In February he escapes from Parma to Verona, where he discovers in the cathedral library the letters of Cicero to Atticus, to his brother Quintus, and to Brutus: this discovery gives him the idea of writing letters to Cicero and to other ancients, and of making a collection of his own letters.

In the autumn he returns to Provence: he will spend most of the next two years at Vaucluse.

1346   He writes *De vita solitaria*, a treatise on the advantages of the secluded rural life, and commences a collection of Latin eclogues, his *Bucolicum carmen*.

1347   After a visit to his brother at the monastery of Montrieux he writes *De otio religiosorum*, a treatise on the virtues and advantages of monastic life.

Either in this or the preceding year, the three sonnets directed against the Papal Court were composed (CXXXVI–CXXXVIII), and a second draft of the *Canzoniere* was made: it probably contained some 130 poems, divided into two sections.

He gives his full support to Cola di Rienzo, who, in his attempt to reform the constitution of Rome, establishes himself as dictator there: Petrarch withdraws his support only when Cola exceeds his powers and is compelled to abdicate under combined pressure from the Pope and the noble Roman families.

1348   In January the Black Death reaches Avignon, and on April 6th Laura dies. Petrarch is at the time in Parma and does not learn of her death until May. Parma is now in the power of the Visconti, and Petrarch enters into correspondence with Luchino Visconti. He spends most of the year at Parma. He begins the *Triumphus Mortis*, and the canzone, *Che debb'io far?* (CCLXVIII).

1349-50 He remains in Northern Italy, principally at Parma, Padua and Mantua. At Padua he receives, through the agency of the ruler, Jacopo da Carrara, a canonry, and with it a house. At Mantua he is the guest of the ruling Gonzaga family.

He writes the *Triumphus Fame* and begins work on a collection of his letters.

1350 Since this is the year of Jubilee, he make a pilgrimage to Rome in the autumn. En route he stops in Florence, and there meets Boccaccio; the two from now onwards will maintain regular correspondence, and Boccaccio will pay Petrarch several visits.

Petrarch returns to Northern Italy near the end of the year.

1351 He is summoned back to Provence by the Pope, who wishes to offer him the post of Papal Secretary: Petrarch declines.

He continues work on the *De viris illustribus* at Vaucluse.

1352 He becomes involved at Avignon in a dispute with one of the papal doctors, and writes the first of a series of *Invective contra medicum*, a work to be completed some time later in Milan.

1353 In early summer Petrarch leaves Provence for good. He travels to Milan, and, somewhat to the disapproval of his more republican-minded friends, accepts the patronage of the Visconti; they present him with a house near the church of Sant'Ambrogio in Milan.

Petrarch will spend most of the next eight years there.

1354   He visits Venice on behalf of the Visconti, becomes acquainted with the Doge, Andrea Dandalo, and attempts to bring about peaceful relations between Venice and Milan.

He begins the *De remediis utriusque fortune*, a treatise on the dangers of good and bad fortune and on the remedies to be applied. In December he visits the Emperor Charles IV, to whom he has previously written several letters urging him to come to Italy, and who is now in residence at Mantua prior to his coronation at Milan early the next year.

1355   To Petrarch's disappointment Charles leaves Italy in June.

Petrarch composes his *Invectiva contra quendam magni status hominem sed nulli scientie aut virtutis*, a diatribe against a cardinal who had accused him of being a poor writer and a flatterer of tyrants.

1356   He makes a journey to the Emperor at Prague on behalf of Galeazzo and Bernabò Visconti: Charles makes him Count Palatine.

1357   He revises *De otio religiosorum*, now become *De otio religioso*, reaches the tenth book of his collection of letters, and revises some of his other works.

1358   He composes the *Itinerarium syriacum*, a guide-book for a friend about to go on pilgrimage to the Holy Land, and completes a third version of the *Canzoniere* (some 170 poems).

1359	He acquires a new house in Milan, just outside the north wall of the city.
1360	He completes the first draft of *De remediis utriusque fortune*.
1361	Early in the year he travels to Paris on behalf of Galeazzo Visconti, and delivers an oration in the presence of the king, John II. In the summer he moves to Padua. He resumes work on the *De vita solitaria*, more or less completes the first collection of letters, the *Epistole familiares*, and commences a second collection, the *Epistole seniles*: he also completes a fourth form of the *Canzoniere* (215 poems).
1362	He moves from Padua to Venice: he proposes to leave his books on his death to the state of Venice as the nucleus of a public library.
1362–70	He divides his time between Venice, Padua and Pavia. This last had been captured by the Visconti in 1359, and apparently Galeazzo Visconti rented a house for Petrarch there.
1366	He completes at Pavia the *De remediis utriusque fortune*: his secretary, Giovanni Malpaghini, finishes copying the *Epistole familiares*, which now consists of 350 letters divided into 24 books. Petrarch turns to a fifth version of the *Canzoniere*.
1367	He writes at Pavia *De sui ipsius et multorum ignorantia*, an invective defending his own attitude to philosophy and criticising the Aristotelianism of the Schools.

1368   Two sonnets written at this time (CXCIV, CXCVI), both of which represent Laura as living, were probably Petrarch's last.

1368-9   He does more work on the *De viris illustribus*, which he dedicates to Francesco da Carrara, ruler of Padua. In return he is given a plot of land at Arquà in the Euganean hills: he has a house built there.

1370-4   He spends most of his last years at Arquà. There he completes the revision of the *Canzoniere*: the last poem to be written was probably the canzone to the Virgin, which was composed in 1373. He puts the finishing touches to the *De vita solitaria* in 1371, and continues work on the *Triumphs*, the *Epistole seniles*, and the *De viris illustribus*, none of which is ever completed.

1373   He writes his last invective, the *Invectiva contra eum qui maledixit Italie*, in which he defends the glories and rights of Italy against the claims of France, especially its claim to the Papacy, which after a brief sojourn in Rome was once again back in Avignon.
                In September he goes on his final diplomatic mission: he is a member of the embassy sent by Francesco da Carrara to Venice, with which he is at war.

1374 July 18th Petrarch dies at Arquà. It is there that he is buried.

Note: This summary is intended to give some idea of Petrarch's travels, his relations with important figures of his time, and of the chronology and content of his works. For more detailed information concerning his life the reader is referred to E. H. Wilkins, *Life of Petrarch* (University of Chicago Press, 1961), and to the three volumes by the same author dealing with particular periods of Petrarch's life: *Studies in the life and works of Petrarch* (1955), *Petrarch's Eight Years in Milan* (1958), *Petrarch's Later Years* (1959), all published by the Mediaeval Academy of America.

For the chronology of the *Canzoniere*, see note on page 57. For the chronology of the Latin writings of Petrarch, see the notes appended to Francesco Petrarca: *Prose*, ed. G. Martellotti, P. G. Ricci, E. Carrara and E. Bianchi (Milan–Naples, 1955).

NOTES ON SOME VERSE-FORMS USED BY PETRARCH

THE CANZONE

Italian canzoni are of two main types. In both each stanza is divisible into a *frons* (Ital. *fronte*) and a *sirima* (Ital. *sirma* or *coda*), and in both the *frons* is further divisible into two *pedes* (Ital. *piedi*). In one of the two types the *sirima* may in turn be divided into two *voltae* (Ital. *volte*); but in the other type, which is the one used by Petrarch, the *sirima* is not so divided. Here is an example of a stanza from a canzone by Petrarch:

	Pes 1	Chiare, fresche e dolci acque	a
		ove le belle membra	b
Frons		pose colei che sola a me par donna;	C
	Pes 2	gentil ramo, ove piacque	a
		(con sospir mi rimembra)	b
		a lei di far al bel fianco colonna;	C
	Diesis:	erba e fior, che la gonna	c
		leggiadra ricoverse	d
		co l'angelico seno;	e
Sirima		aer sacro sereno,	e
		ove amor co' begli occhi il cor m'aperse:	D
	Final Couplet	date udienzia insieme	f
		a le dolenti mie parole estreme.	F

The number of stanzas and the number of lines in a stanza may vary from canzone to canzone, as may the distribution of hendecasyllables and heptasyllables. Within a canzone, however, all stanzas must be equal. Moreover, as in the stanza above, each *pes* in the stanza must be equal to the other in the number of lines it contains, and the lines in the first *pes* must correspond in length to those in the second. The lines of a *pes* will rhyme either with other lines in that *pes* or (as here) with lines in the other *pes*. The *sirima* begins with a line known as the *diesis* (Ital. *diesi*) which binds it in rhyme to the last line of the *frons*. The *sirima* ends with two lines which rhyme with each other. If we use a small letter for the heptasyllables and a capital for the hendecasyllables, the rhyme-scheme of the above stanza can be summarised as abC.abC.cdeeDfF. Since this pattern has to be repeated in the other stanzas, the second stanza in the same poem will give us ghI.ghI.ilmmLnN, and so on. At the end of a canzone there is usually a *congedo* or *commiato* or *tornata* in which the poet takes leave of his own composition. In the poem from which we have quoted above, this reads as follows:

> Se tu avessi ornamenti quant'hai voglia,   Y
> potresti arditamente   z
> uscir del bosco e gir in fra la gente.   Z

This corresponds in form to a section of the *sirima* (in this case the last three lines).

THE SESTINA

The canzone sestina or sestina lirica has six indivisible six-line stanzas plus a three-line *tornata*, all composed of hendeca-syllables. Instead of rhymes, the sestina has the words which end the lines of the first stanza repeated in different order at the end of the lines of the following stanzas. If the reader will look at the sestina by Petrarch beginning *A qualunque animale alberga in terra* (no. 5 in this collection) he will see that the rhyme-words in it follow the scheme 1. ABCDEF; 2. FAEBDC; 3. CFDABE; 4. ECBFAD; 5. DEACFB; 6. BDFECA. This means that each stanza after the first repeats the rhyme-words of the preceding stanza in the order 615243 (i.e. starting from the extremities of the stanza and working inwards). Although the *tornata* is of three lines only, it contains all six rhyme-words, two being placed in each line, one intern-ally and one at the end. Usually the rhyme-words in the *tornata* either follow directly in the order 123456 or, moving from the extremities inwards, 162534. But other orders are admissible, and in the poem referred to in this note the order is 153462.

THE SONNET

The Petrarchan or Italian sonnet consists of fourteen hendeca-syllables divided into two quatrains and two tercets, unlike the English or Shakespearean sonnet, which is composed of three quatrains and a final couplet. The quatrains usually follow the rhyme-scheme ABAB. ABAB or ABBA. ABBA; but Pet-ràrch in the sonnet *Se lamentar augelli* (no. 42 in this selection) has ABAB. BABA. The tercets either have two rhymes used thrice or three rhymes used twice e.g. CDC.DCD or CDE.CDE, or CDC.CDC, or CDD.CDD. Indeed, any combination is possible, provided that at least one of the rhymes in the first tercet finds a corresponding rhyme in the second. Petrarch is fond of the variant CDE.DCE. Only once does he use CDE.EDC—in *Più volte amor* (XCIII).

THE MADRIGAL

The madrigale enjoys considerable variety of form. It generally consists of two *pedes* (each composed of three hendecasyllables), followed by a final rhyming couplet (also hendecasyllabic). It may, however, have three *pedes*, or it may have two couplets. For an example, see *Non al suo amante* (no. 9 in this collection). It consists of eight lines (two *pedes* and a couplet) with the rhyme-scheme ABA.BCB.CC. Petrarch also used the schemes ABC.ABC.DD; ABB.ACC.CDD; and ABA.CBC.DE.DE.

The student who requires further information on versification is referred to R. Spongano, *Nozioni ed esempi di metrica italiana* (Bologna, 1966), and W. Theodor Elwert, *Versificazione italiana dalle origini ai giorni nostri* (Florence, 1973).

A NOTE ON THE CHRONOLOGY
AND THE TEXT

We have not attempted to give an account of the extremely complicated problem of the chronology of Petrarch's *Canzoniere*, not merely because adequate discussion of it would require treatment much more lengthy than our introduction, but because the student will find a full study of it in E. H. Wilkins, *The Making of the 'Canzoniere' and other Petrarchan Studies* (Rome, 1951), which will also provide him with descriptions of the two most important manuscripts of Petrarch's Italian poems, Vat. Lat. 3195 and 3196, and a classification of other manuscripts.

In the presentation of the works of Italian writers of the Middle Ages and Renaissance to the modern reader, it is customary to make changes in spelling and punctuation in order to bring the text nearer the conventions of Italian orthography in our time. That has been done in the texts presented in this anthology (and we hope that our attempts at punctuation, in which we differ somewhat from the editions known to us, will make the poems easier, not more difficult to read). This means that the student who read a diplomatic edition would find, in the case of the first sonnet of our anthology, not the text we have given, but the following:

U Oi chafcoltate in rime fparfe il fuono
Di quei fofpiri ondio nudriual core
In ful mio primo giouenile errore
Quãdera ĩ parte altruom da q̃l chi fono
Del uario ftile inchio piango z ragiono
Frale uane fperançe / el uan dolore
Oue fĩa chi p proua intenda amore
Spero trouar pieta . non che perdono .
Ma ben ueggio or fĩ come al popol tutto
Fauola fui gran tẽpo . onde fouente
Di me medefmo meco mi uergogno .
Et del mio uaneggiar uergogna el frutto
El penterfĩ / el conofcer chiaramẽte
Che quãto piace almõdo e breue fogno .

The reader who is interested in knowing exactly what degree of change is involved in particular poems will find such a diplomatic edition in *Francisci Petrarche laureati poete Rerum vulgarium fragmenta*, ed. E. Modigliani (Rome, 1904), and if he wishes to see what Vat. Lat. 3195 looks like, he can do so in *L'originale del Canzoniere di Francesco Petrarca, Codice Vaticano Latino 3195, riprodotto in fototipia* a cura della Biblioteca Vaticana, ed. M. Vattasso (Milan, 1905). A few lines in Petrarch's hand are reproduced as a frontispiece to the present volume. For other relevant works, he should see Wilkins, *op. cit.*, esp. pp. xiv–xv. For a philologically rigorous modern edition intended for those who wish to study the language and punctuation of the original, he should refer to the *Rerum vulgarium fragmenta*, ed. G. Contini (Paris, 1949).

BIBLIOGRAPHICAL NOTE

The student of Petrarch will not suffer from lack of biblio-
graphical information; his difficulty will be to know where to
begin. We have already indicated in the notes a number of
works which can be read in connection with particular problems. Here we shall merely name a few books which can serve
as starting-points in various fields and in whose bibliographies
the student who wishes to pursue his studies in those fields
will find further suggestions.

Notable modern editions are *Il Canzoniere*, ed. G. Contini,
6th edition (Turin, 1975), and *Le Rime sparse e i Trionfi*, ed. E.
Chiòrboli (Bari, 1930). Two useful volumes for the student are
the *Rime, Trionfi e poesie latine*, ed. F. Neri, G. Martellotti,
E. Bianchi and N. Sapegno (Milan–Naples, 1951), and *Prose*,
ed. G. Martellotti, P. G. Ricci, E. Carrara and E. Bianchi
(Milan–Naples, 1955); the editors have provided an Italian
translation of those Latin works by Petrarch which they have
included. The National Edition of Petrarch is as yet incom-
plete, but the following volumes have appeared in it: *L'Africa*,
ed. N. Festa (Florence 1926; Nat. Ed., Vol. I); *Le familiari*,
Vols. I–III, ed. V. Rossi, and Vol. IV, ed. V. Rossi and U.
Bosco (Florence 1933–42; Nat. Ed., Vols. X–XIII); *Rerum
memorandarum libri*, ed. G. Billanovich (Florence 1945; Nat.
Ed., Vol. XIV). There are some modern editions of other Latin
works of Petrarch's; for those works not in modern editions we
can have recourse to the complete editions published at Basle
in 1554 and 1581.

As for works on Petrarch, the following will serve as a
beginning:

U. Bosco, *Francesco Petrarca*, Bari, 1961.

C. Calcaterra, 'Il Petrarca e il petrarchismo' in *Problemi e
orientamenti di letteratura italiana*, ed. A. Momigliano, Vol.
III, Milan, 1949.

F. De Sanctis, *Saggio sul Petrarca*, Bari, 1954.

Leonard Forster, *The Icy Fire*, Cambridge, 1969.

P. de Nolhac, *Pétrarque et l'humanisme*, Paris, 1907.

A. Enzo Quaglio, *Francesco Petrarca*, Milan, 1967 (with very good bibliography, including a list of Petrarch bibliographies).

B. T. Sozzi, *Petrarca*, Palermo, 1963 (with useful bibliographies).

J. H. Whitfield, *Petrarch and the Renascence*, Oxford, 1943.

E. H. Wilkins, *Life of Petrarch*, Chicago, 1961.

E. H. Wilkins, *The making of the 'Canzoniere' and other Petrarchan studies*, Rome, 1951.

E. H. Wilkins, *Studies in the life and works of Petrarch*, Cambridge, Mass., 1955.

SELECTED POEMS

I (1)

Voi ch'ascoltate in rime sparse il suono
di quei sospiri ond'io nudriva 'l core
in sul mio primo giovenile errore,
4   quand'era in parte altr'uom da quel ch'i' sono:

del vario stile in ch'io piango e ragiono,
fra le vane speranze e 'l van dolore,
ove sia chi per prova intenda amore,
8   spero trovar pietà, non che perdono.

Ma ben veggio or sí come al popol tutto
favola fui gran tempo, onde sovente
11   di me medesmo meco mi vergogno;

e del mio vaneggiar vergogna è 'l frutto
e 'l pentersi, e 'l conoscer chiaramente
14   che quanto piace al mondo è breve sogno.

2 (III)

Era il giorno ch' al sol si scoloraro
per la pietà del suo fattore i rai,
quando i' fui preso, e non me ne guardai,
4   che i be' vostr' occhi, donna, mi legaro.

Tempo non mi parea da far riparo
contr' a' colpi d'amor; però m' andai
secur, senza sospetto; onde i miei guai
8   nel comune dolor s'incominciaro.

Trovommi amor del tutto disarmato,
et aperta la via per gli occhi al core,
11   che di lagrime son fatti uscio e varco.

Però, al mio parer, non li fu onore
ferir me de saetta in quello stato,
14   a voi armata non mostrar pur l'arco.

3 (XII)

Se la mia vita da l'aspro tormento
si può tanto schermire e dagli affanni,
ch'i' veggia per vertú degli ultimi anni,
4   donna, de' be' vostr' occhi il lume spento,

e i cape' d'oro fin farsi d'argento,
e lassar le ghirlande e i verdi panni,
e 'l viso scolorir, che ne' miei danni
8   a lamentar mi fa pauroso e lento,

pur mi darà tanta baldanza amore,
ch'i' vi discovrirò de' miei martiri
11   qua' sono stati gli anni e i giorni e l'ore,

e se 'l tempo è contrario ai be' desiri,
non fia ch'almen non giunga al mio dolore
14   alcun soccorso di tardi sospiri.

4 (XVI)

Movesi il vecchierel canuto e bianco
del dolce loco ov' ha sua età fornita
e da la famigliuola sbigottita
4   che vede il caro padre venir manco;

indi traendo poi l'antico fianco
per l'estreme giornate di sua vita,
quanto piú po, col buon voler s'aita,
8   rotto dagli anni e dal cammino stanco;

e viene a Roma, seguendo 'l desio,
per mirar la sembianza di Colui
11   ch'ancor lassú nel ciel vedere spera:

cosí, lasso, talor vo cercand'io,
donna, quanto è possibile in altrui
14   la disiata vostra forma vera.

5 (XXII)

A qualunque animale alberga in terra,
se non se alquanti c'hanno in odio il sole,
tempo da travagliare è quanto è 'l giorno;
ma poi che 'l ciel accende le sue stelle,
qual torna a casa e qual s'annida in selva
6   per aver posa almeno infin a l'alba.

Et io, da che comincia la bella alba
a scuoter l'ombra intorno de la terra,
svegliando gli animali in ogni selva,
non ho mai triegua di sospir col sole;
poi, quand'io veggio fiammeggiar le stelle,
12   vo lagrimando e disiando il giorno.

Quando la sera scaccia il chiaro giorno,
e le tenebre nostre altrui fanno alba,
miro pensoso le crudeli stelle
che m'hanno fatto di sensibil terra,
e maledico il dí ch' i' vidi 'l sole;
18   che mi fa in vista un uom nudrito in selva.

Non credo che pascesse mai per selva
sí aspra fera, o di notte o di giorno,
come costei ch'i' piango a l'ombra e al sole,
e non mi stanca primo sonno od alba,
ché, ben ch'i' sia mortal corpo di terra,
24   lo mio fermo desir vien da le stelle.

Prima ch' i' torni a voi, lucenti stelle,
o tomi giú ne l'amorosa selva
lassando il corpo che fia trita terra,
vedess' io in lei pietà, che 'n un sol giorno
può ristorar molt'anni, e 'nanzi l'alba
30   puommi arricchir dal tramontar del sole.

Con lei foss' io da che si parte il sole
e non ci vedess'altri che le stelle,
sol una notte, e mai non fosse l'alba!
E non se transformasse in verde selva
per uscirmi di braccia, come il giorno
36   ch' Apollo la seguia qua giú per terra.

Ma io sarò sotterra in secca selva,
e 'l giorno andrà pien di minute stelle
39   prima ch' a sí dolce alba arrivi il sole.

6 (XXIII)

Nel dolce tempo de la prima etade,
che nascer vide, ed ancor quasi in erba,
la fera voglia che per mio mal crebbe,
perché, cantando, il duol si disacerba,
5 canterò com' io vissi in libertade
mentre amor nel mio albergo a sdegno s'ebbe;
poi seguirò sí come a lui ne 'ncrebbe
troppo altamente, e che di ciò m'avvenne,
di ch' io son fatto a molta gente essempio;
10 ben che 'l mio duro scempio
sia scritto altrove, sí che mille penne
ne son già stanche, e quasi in ogni valle
rimbombi il suon de' miei gravi sospiri,
ch' acquistan fede a la penosa vita.
15 E se qui la memoria non m'aita,
come suol fare, iscusilla i martiri
et un penser, che solo angoscia dàlle,
tal ch' ad ogni altro fa voltar le spalle,
e mi face obliar me stesso a forza;
20 ch' e' ten di me quel d'entro, et io la scorza.

I' dico che dal dí che 'l primo assalto
mi diede amor, molt' anni eran passati,
sí ch' io cangiava il giovenil aspetto;
e d'intorno al mio cor pensier gelati
25 fatto avean quasi adamantino smalto
ch' allentar non lassava il duro affetto;
lagrima ancor non mi bagnava il petto
né rompea il sonno, e quel che in me non era
mi pareva un miracolo in altrui.
30 Lasso, che son? che fui?
La vita el fin, e 'l dí loda la sera.
Ché, sentendo il crudel di ch'io ragiono
infin allor percossa di suo strale

non essermi passato oltra la gonna,
35 prese in sua scorta una possente donna,
ver cui poco già mai mi valse o vale
ingegno o forza o dimandar perdono:
ei duo mi trasformaro in quel ch' i' sono,
facendomi d'uom vivo un lauro verde
40 che per fredda stagion foglia non perde.

Qual mi fec'io, quando primier m'accorsi
de la trasfigurata mia persona,
e i capei vidi far di quella fronde
di che sperato avea già lor corona,
45 e i piedi in ch' io mi stetti e mossi e corsi
(com'ogni membro a l'anima risponde)
diventar due radici sovra l'onde
non di Peneo, ma d'un piú altero fiume,
e 'n duo rami mutarsi ambe le braccia!
50 Né meno ancor m'agghiaccia
l'esser coverto poi di bianche piume,
allor che fulminato e morto giacque
il mio sperar che tropp'alto montava;
ché, perch' io non sapea dove né quando
55 me 'l ritrovasse, solo, lagrimando,
là 've tolto mi fu, dí e notte andava
ricercando dallato e dentro a l'acque;
e giammai poi la mia lingua non tacque,
mentre poteo, del suo cader maligno;
60 ond'io presi col suon color d'un cigno.

Cosí lungo l'amate rive andai,
che volendo parlar, cantava sempre
mercé chiamando con estrania voce:
né mai in sí dolci o in sí soavi tempre
65 risonar seppi gli amorosi guai
che 'l cor s'umiliasse aspro e feroce.
Qual fu a sentir, ché 'l ricordar mi coce?

Ma molto piú di quel ch'è per inanzi,
de la dolce et acerba mia nemica
70 è bisogno ch'io dica,
ben che sia tal ch'ogni parlare avanzi.
Questa che col mirar gli animi fura,
m'aperse il petto, e 'l cor prese con mano,
dicendo a me: «Di ciò non far parola».
75 Poi la rividi in altro abito sola,
tal ch' i' non la conobbi, o senso umano!
anzi le dissi 'l ver, pien di paura,
ed ella ne l'usata sua figura
tosto tornando, fecemi, oimè lasso,
80 d'un quasi vivo e sbigottito sasso.

Ella parlava sí turbata in vista
che tremar mi fea dentro a quella petra,
udendo: «I' non son forse chi tu credi».
E dicea meco: «Se costei mi spetra,
85 nulla vita mi fia noiosa o trista:
a farmi lagrimar, signor mio, riedi».
Come non so, pur io mossi indi i piedi,
non altrui incolpando che me stesso,
mezzo, tutto quel dí, tra vivo e morto.
90 Ma perché 'l tempo è corto,
la penna al buon voler non po gir presso,
onde piú cose ne la mente scritte
vo trapassando, e sol d'alcune parlo,
che meraviglia fanno a chi l'ascolta.
95 Morte mi s'era intorno al cor avvolta;
né tacendo potea di sua man trarlo
o dar soccorso a le vertuti afflitte,
le vive voci m'erano interditte;
ond'io gridai con carta e con incostro:
100 «Non son mio, no; s'io moro, il danno è vostro.»

Ben mi credea dinanzi agli occhi suoi
d'indegno far cosí di mercé degno,

e questa spene m'avea fatto ardito.
Ma talora umiltà spegne disdegno,
105 talor l'enfiamma, e ciò sepp'io da poi
lunga stagion di tenebre vestito,
ch' a quei preghi il mio lume era sparito,
ed io, non ritrovando intorno intorno
ombra di lei, né pur de' suoi piedi orma,
110 come uom che tra via dorma,
gittaimi stanco sovra l'erba un giorno.
Ivi, accusando il fuggitivo raggio,
a le lagrime triste allargai 'l freno,
e lasciaile cader come a lor parve;
115 né già mai neve sotto al sol disparve,
com'io senti' me tutto venir meno,
e farmi una fontana a piè d'un faggio;
gran tempo umido tenni quel viaggio:
chi udí mai d'uom vero nascer fonte?
120 E parlo cose manifeste e conte.

L'alma ch'è sol da Dio fatta gentile,
ché già d'altrui non po venir tal grazia,
simile al suo fattor stato ritene;
però di perdonar mai non è sazia
125 a chi col core e col sembiante umile,
dopo quantunque offese a mercé vene.
E se contra suo stile ella sostene
d'esser molto pregata, in lui si specchia,
e fal perché 'l peccar piú si pavente,
130 ché non ben si ripente
de l'un mal chi de l'altro s'apparecchia.
Poi che madonna da pietà commossa
degnò mirarme, e ricognovve e vide
gir di pari la pena col peccato,
135 benigna mi redusse al primo stato.
Ma nulla ha 'l mondo in ch'uom saggio si fide;
ch'ancor poi, ripregando, i nervi e l'ossa
mi volse in dura selce, e cosí scossa

voce rimasi de l'antiche some,
140 chiamando morte e lei sola per nome.

Spirto doglioso errante (mi rimembra)
per spelunche deserte e pellegrine
piansi molt'anni il mio sfrenato ardire,
et ancor poi trovai di quel mal fine,
145 e ritornai ne le terrene membra,
credo, per piú dolore ivi sentire.
I' segui' tanto avanti il mio desire,
ch'un dí, cacciando sí com'io solea,
mi mossi, e quella fera bella e cruda
150 in una fonte ignuda
si stava, quando 'l sol piú forte ardea.
Io, perché d'altra vista non m'appago,
stetti a mirarla, ond'ella ebbe vergogna,
e per farne vendetta o per celarse,
155 l'acqua nel viso co le man mi sparse.
Vero dirò, forse e' parrà menzogna,
ch' i' senti' trarmi de la propria imago,
et in un cervo solitario e vago
di selva in selva ratto mi trasformo,
160 et ancor de' miei can fuggo lo stormo.

Canzon, i' non fu' mai quel nuvol d'oro
che poi discese in preziosa pioggia,
sí che 'l foco di Giove in parte spense;
ma fui ben fiamma ch'un bel guardo accense
165 e fui l'uccel che piú per l'aere poggia,
alzando lei che ne' miei detti onoro;
né per nova figura il primo alloro
seppi lassar, ché pur la sua dolce ombra
169 ogni men bel piacer del cor mi sgombra.

7 (XXXV)

Solo e pensoso i piú deserti campi
vo mesurando a passi tardi e lenti,
e gli occhi porto per fuggire intenti
4   ove vestigio uman l'arena stampi.

Altro schermo non trovo che mi scampi
dal manifesto accorger de le genti;
perché negli atti d'allegrezza spenti
8   di fuor si legge com'io dentro avvampi;

sí ch'io mi credo omai che monti e piagge
e fiumi e selve sappian di che tempre
11   sia la mia vita, ch'è celata altrui.

Ma pur sí aspre vie né sí selvagge
cercar non so, ch' amor non venga sempre
14   ragionando con meco, et io con lui.

8 (L)

Ne la stagion che 'l ciel rapido inchina
verso occidente e che 'l dí nostro vola
a gente che di là forse l'aspetta,
veggendosi in lontan paese sola
la stanca vecchiarella pellegrina
6   raddoppia i passi, e piú e piú s'affretta;
e poi cosí soletta
al fin di sua giornata
talora è consolata
10   d'alcun breve riposo, ov'ella oblia
la noia e 'l mal de la passata via.
Ma, lasso, ogni dolor che 'l dí m'adduce
cresce qualor s'invia
14   per partirsi da noi l'eterna luce.

Come 'l sol volge le 'nfiammate rote
per dar luogo a la notte, onde discende
dagli altissimi monti maggior l'ombra,
l'avaro zappador l'arme riprende,
e con parole e con alpestri note
20   ogni gravezza del suo petto sgombra;
e poi la mensa ingombra
di povere vivande,
simili a quelle ghiande
le qua' fuggendo tutto 'l mondo onora.
25   Ma chi vuol si rallegri ad ora ad ora,
ch' i' pur non ebbi ancor, non dirò lieta,
ma riposata un'ora,
28   né per volger di ciel né di pianeta.

Quando vede 'l pastor calare i raggi
del gran pianeta al nido ov'egli alberga
e 'mbrunir le contrade d'oriente,
drizzasi in piedi e co l'usata verga,

lassando l'erba e le fontane e i faggi,
34 move la schiera sua soavemente;
poi lontan da la gente,
o casetta o spelunca
di verdi frondi ingiunca;
ivi senza pensier s'adagia e dorme.
39 Ahi, crudo amor! ma tu allor piú m'informe
a seguir d'una fera che mi strugge
la voce e i passi e l'orme,
42 e lei non stringi che s'appiatta e fugge.

E i naviganti in qualche chiusa valle
gettan le membra, poi che 'l sol s'asconde,
sul duro legno e sotto a l'aspre gonne.
Ma io, perché s'attuffi in mezzo l'onde,
e lasci Ispagna dietro a le sue spalle
48 e Granata e Marrocco e le Colonne,
e gli uomini e le donne
e 'l mondo e gli animali
acquetino i lor mali,
fine non pongo al mio ostinato affanno,
53 e duolmi ch'ogni giorno arroge al danno:
ch' i' son già, pur crescendo in questa voglia,
ben presso al decim' anno,
56 né poss'indovinar chi me ne scioglia.

E perché un poco nel parlar mi sfogo,
veggio la sera i buoi tornare sciolti
da le campagne e da' solcati colli.
I miei sospiri a me perché non tolti
quando che sia? perché no 'l grave giogo?
62 perché dí e notte gli occhi miei son molli?
Misero me, che volli,
quando primier sí fiso
gli tenni nel bel viso,
per iscolpirlo, imaginando, in parte
67 onde mai né per forza né per arte

mosso sarà, fin ch' i' sia dato in preda
a chi tutto diparte?
70   Né so ben anco che di lei mi creda.

Canzon, se l'esser meco
dal mattino a la sera
t'ha fatto di mia schiera,
tu non vorrai mostrarti in ciascun loco,
e d'altrui loda curerai sí poco,
76   ch' assai ti fia pensar di poggio in poggio
come m'ha concio 'l foco
78   di questa viva petra ov' io m'appoggio.

9 (LII)

Non al suo amante piú Diana piacque
quando, per tal ventura, tutta ignuda
la vide in mezzo de le gelide acque,

4   ch' a me la pastorella alpestra e cruda
posta a bagnar un leggiadretto velo,
ch' a l'aura il vago e biondo capel chiuda;

8   tal che mi fece, or quand' egli arde 'l cielo,
tutto tremar d'un amoroso gelo.

IO (LIII)

Spirto gentil che quelle membra reggi
dentro a le qua' peregrinando alberga
un signor valoroso, accorto e saggio,
poi che se' giunto a l'onorata verga
colla qual Roma e suoi erranti correggi,
6   e la richiami al suo antiquo viaggio:
io parló a te, però ch' altrove un raggio
non veggio di vertú, ch' al mondo è spenta,
né trovo chi di mal far si vergogni.
Che s' aspetti non so, né che s' agogni
11   Italia, che suoi guai non par che senta;
vecchia, oziosa e lenta,
dormirà sempre, e non fia chi la svegli?
14   Le man l' avess' io avvolto entro' capegli!

Non spero che giammai dal pigro sonno
mova la testa, per chiamar ch' uom faccia,
sí gravemente è oppressa e di tal soma.
Ma non senza destino a le tue braccia,
che scuoter forte e sollevar la ponno,
20   è or commesso il nostro capo Roma.
Pon man in quella venerabil chioma
securamente e ne le trecce sparte,
sí che la neghittosa esca del fango.
I' che dí e notte del suo strazio piango,
25   di mia speranza ho in te la maggior parte:
ché se 'l popol di Marte
devesse al proprio onore alzar mai gli occhi,
28   parmi pur ch' a' tuoi dí la grazia tocchi.

L'antiche mura ch' ancor teme ed ama
e trema 'l mondo, quando si rimembra
del tempo andato e 'ndietro si rivolve,
e i sassi dove fur chiuse le membra

di ta' che non saranno senza fama
34   se l'universo pria non si dissolve:
e tutto quel ch' una ruina involve,
per te spera saldar ogni suo vizio.
O grandi Scipioni, o fedel Bruto,
quanto v' aggrada s' egli è ancor venuto
39   romor là giú del ben locato offizio!
Come cre' che Fabrizio
si faccia lieto udendo la novella,
42   e dice: «Roma mia sarà ancor bella.»

E se cosa di qua nel ciel si cura,
l'anime che lassú son cittadine
et hanno i corpi abandonati in terra,
del lungo odio civil ti pregan fine,
per cui la gente ben non s'assecura,
48   onde 'l camin a' lor tetti si serra,
che fur già sí devoti, et ora in guerra
quasi spelunca di ladron son fatti,
tal ch' a' buon solamente uscio si chiude,
e tra gli altari e tra le statue ignude
53   ogni impresa crudel par che si tratti.
Deh, quanto diversi atti!
Né senza squille s'incomincia assalto,
56   che per Dio ringraziar fur poste in alto.

Le donne lagrimose e 'l vulgo inerme
de la tenera etate e i vecchi stanchi,
ch'hanno sé in odio e la soverchia vita,
e i neri fraticelli e i bigi e i bianchi,
coll'altre schiere travagliate e 'nferme,
62   gridan: «O signor nostro, aita, aita!»
E la povera gente sbigottita
ti scopre le sue piaghe a mille a mille,
ch' Anibale, non ch' altri, farian pio;
e se ben guardi a la magion di Dio

67 ch' arde oggi tutta, assai poche faville
spegnendo, fien tranquille
le voglie che si mostran sí 'nfiammate:
70 onde fien l'opre tue nel ciel laudate.

Orsi, lupi, leoni, aquile e serpi
ad una gran marmorea colonna
fanno noia sovente et a sé danno.
Di costor piange quella gentil donna
75 che t'ha chiamato, a ciò che di lei sterpi
le male piante che fiorir non sanno.
Passato è già piú che 'l millesimo anno
che 'n lei mancar quell'anime leggiadre
che locata l'avean là dov' ell' era.
Ahi, nova gente oltra misura altera,
81 irreverente a tanta ed a tal madre!
Tu marito, tu padre:
ogni soccorso di tua man s' attende,
84 ché 'l maggior padre ad altr' opera intende.

Rade volte adiven ch' a l'alte imprese
fortuna ingiuriosa non contrasti,
ch' a gli animosi fatti mal s' accorda;
ora, sgombrando 'l passo onde tu intrasti,
fammisi perdonar molt' altre offese,
90 ch' al men qui da se stessa si discorda:
però che quanto 'l mondo si ricorda,
ad uom mortal no fu aperta la via
per farsi, come a te, di fama eterno:
che puoi drizzar, s' i' non falso discerno,
95 in stato la piú nobil monarchia.
Quanta gloria ti fia
dir: «Gli altri l'aitar giovene e forte;
98 questi in vecchiezza la scampò da morte!»

Sopra 'l monte Tarpeio, canzon, vedrai
un cavalier ch'Italia tutta onora,
pensoso piú d'altrui che di se stesso.
Digli: «Un che non ti vide ancor da presso,
103   se non come per fama uom s'innamora,
dice che Roma ogni ora,
con gli occhi di dolor bagnati e molli,
106   ti chier mercé da tutti sette i colli.»

[handwritten:] Sonnet. 14 hendecasyllables - 2 quatrains 2 tercets.

[handwritten:] A Benediction of love Painful & Pleasant

I I (LXI)

[handwritten:] Blessed

Benedetto sia 'l giorno e 'l mese e l'anno **A**
e la stagione e 'l tempo e l'ora e 'l punto **B** *[handwritten: point]*
e 'l bel paese e 'l loco ov'io fui giunto **B** *[handwritten: caught]*

4   da' duo begli occhi che legato m' hanno; **A**

[handwritten: united   sweet   breath anguish]
e benedetto il primo dolce affanno **A**
[handwritten: C] ch' i' ebbi ad esser con amor congiunto, **B**
[handwritten: bow arrows]
e l'arco e le saette ond' i' fui punto, **B**

8   e le piaghe che 'nfin al cor mi vanno. **A**
[handwritten: wounds]

[handwritten: many voices]
Benedette le voci tante ch' io **C**
chiamando il nome de mia donna ho sparte, **D** *[handwritten: divided]*

11   e i sospiri e le lagrime e 'l desio; **C**
[handwritten: sighs laments?]

e benedette sian tutte le carte **D**
ov' io fama l'acquisto, e 'l pensier mio, **C**

14   ch' è sol di lei, sí ch' altra non v'ha parte. **D**
[handwritten: only other   if the other has not left]

[handwritten:] 6 When I was compelled to be joined with love

12 (LXII)

Padre del ciel, dopo i perduti giorni,
dopo le notti vaneggiando spese
con quel fero desio ch' al cor s'accese,
4   mirando gli atti per mio mal sí adorni,

piacciati omai, col tuo lume, ch' io torni
ad altra vita et a piú belle imprese,
sí ch' avendo le reti indarno tese,
8   il mio duro adversario se ne scorni.

Or volge, Signor mio, l'undecimo anno
ch' i' fui sommesso al dispietato giogo
11   che sopra i piú soggetti è piú feroce.

Miserere del mio non degno affanno:
reduci i pensier vaghi a miglior luogo;
14   rammenta lor come oggi fusti in croce.

13 (LXX)

Lasso me, ch' i' non so in qual parte pieghi
la speme ch' è tradita omai piú volte;
ché se non è chi con pietà m'ascolte,
perché sparger al ciel sí spessi preghi?
5 Ma s' egli aven ch' ancor non mi si nieghi
finir anzi 'l mio fine
queste voci meschine,
non gravi al mio signor perch' io il ripreghi
di dir libero un dí tra l'erba e i fiori:
10 «Drez et rayson es qu' ieu ciant e 'm demori».

Ragion è ben ch' alcuna volta io canti,
però c'ho sospirato sí gran tempo,
che mai non incomincio assai per tempo
per adequar col riso i dolor tanti.
15 E s'io potesse far ch' agli occhi santi
porgesse alcun diletto
qualche dolce mio detto,
o me beato sopra gli altri amanti!
Ma piú quand' io dirò senza mentire:
20 «Donna mi priega, per ch' io voglio dire».

Vaghi pensier, che cosí passo passo
scorto m'avete a ragionar tant' alto,
vedete che madonna ha 'l cor di smalto
sí forte ch'io per me dentro nol passo.
25 Ella non degna di mirar sí basso
che di nostre parole
curi, ché 'l ciel non vole,
al qual pur contrastando i' son già lasso;
onde come nel cor m'induro e 'naspro
30 «cosí nel mio parlar voglio esser aspro».

Che parlo? o dove sono? e chi m'inganna
altri ch' io stesso e 'l desiar soverchio?
Già, s' i' trascorro il ciel di cerchio in cerchio,
nessun pianeta a pianger mi condanna;
35   se mortal velo il mio veder appanna,
che colpa è de le stelle
o de le cose belle?
Meco si sta chi dí e notte m' affanna,
poi che del suo piacer mi fe' gir grave
40   «la dolce vista e 'l bel guardo soave».

Tutte le cose di che 'l mondo è adorno
uscir buone de man del mastro eterno;
ma me, che cosí a dentro non discerno,
abbaglia il bel che mi si mostra intorno,
45   e s' al vero splendor già mai ritorno
l' occhio non po star fermo:
cosí l' ha fatto infermo
pur la sua propria colpa, e non quel giorno
ch' i' volsi in ver l' angelica beltade
50   «nel dolce tempo de la prima etade».

14 (LXXII)

Gentil mia donna, i' veggio
nel mover de' vostr' occhi un dolce lume,
che mi mostra la via ch' al ciel conduce;
e per lungo costume,
dentro là dove sol con amor seggio,
6   quasi visibilmente il cor traluce.
Questa è la vista ch' a ben far m' induce
e che mi scorge al glorioso fine;
questa sola dal vulgo m' allontana.
Né già mai lingua umana
11   contar poria quel che le due divine
luci sentir mi fanno,
e quando 'l verno sparge le pruine,
e quando poi ringiovenisce l' anno
15   qual era al tempo del mio primo affanno.

Io penso: «Se là suso,
onde 'l motor eterno de le stelle
degnò mostrar del suo lavoro in terra,
son l' altr' opre sí belle,
aprasi la pregione ov' io son chiuso,
21   e che 'l camino a tal vita mi serra.»
Poi mi rivolgo a la mia usata guerra,
ringraziando natura e 'l dí ch' io nacqui,
che reservato m'hanno a tanto bene,
e lei ch' a tanta spene
26   alzò il mio cor; ché 'nsin allor io giacqui
a me noioso e grave;
da quel dí inanzi a me medesmo piacqui,
empiendo d'un pensier alto e soave
30   quel core ond' hanno i begli occhi la chiave.

Né mai stato gioioso
amor o la volubile fortuna

dieder a chi piú fur nel mondo amici,
ch' i' nol cangiassi ad una
rivolta d'occhi, ond' ogni mio riposo
36   vien come ogni arbor vien da sue radici.
Vaghe faville, angeliche, beatrici
de la mia vita, ove 'l piacer s'accende
che dolcemente mi consuma e strugge;
come sparisce e fugge
41   ogni altro lume dove 'l vostro splende,
cosí de lo mio core,
quando tanta dolcezza in lui discende,
ogni altra cosa, ogni penser va fore,
45   e solo ivi con voi rimanse amore.

Quanta dolcezza unquanco
fu in cor d'avventurosi amanti accolta
tutta in un loco, a quel ch' i' sento è nulla,
quando voi alcuna volta
soavemente tra 'l bel nero e 'l bianco
51   volgete il lume in cui amor si trastulla;
e credo da le fasce e da la culla
al mio imperfetto, a la fortuna avversa,
questo rimedio provedesse il cielo.
Torto mi face il velo,
56   e la man che sí spesso s'attraversa
fra 'l mio sommo diletto
e gli occhi, onde dí e notte si rinversa
il gran desio per isfogare il petto,
60   che forma tien dal variato aspetto.

Perch' io veggio, e mi spiace,
che natural mia dote a me non vale
né mi fa degno d'un sí caro sguardo,
sforzomi d'esser tale
qual a l'alta speranza si conface
66   et al foco gentil ond' io tutto ardo.
S'al ben veloce e al contrario tardo,

dispregiator di quanto 'l mondo brama,
per solicito studio posso farme,
porrebbe forse aitarme
nel benigno iudicio una tal fama.

71

Certo il fin de' miei pianti,
che non altronde il cor doglioso chiama,
ven da' begli occhi al fin dolce tremanti,
ultima speme de' cortesi amanti.

75

Canzon, l'una sorella è poco inanzi,
e l'altra sento in quel medesmo albergo
apparecchiarsi, ond' io piú carta vergo.

78

15 (LXXXI)

Io son sí stanco sotto 'l fascio antico
de le mie colpe e de l' usanza ria,
ch' i' temo forte di mancar tra via
4   e di cader in man del mio nemico.

Ben venne a dilivrarmi un grande amico,
per somma et ineffabil cortesia;
poi volò fuor de la veduta mia,
8   sí ch' a mirarlo indarno m'affatico.

Ma la sua voce ancor qua giú rimbomba:
«O voi che travagliate, ecco 'l camino;
11   venite a me, se 'l passo altri non serra».

Qual grazia, qual amore o qual destino
mi darà penne in guisa di colomba,
14   ch' i' mi riposi e levimi da terra?

16 (XC)

Erano i capei d'oro a l'aura sparsi,
che 'n mille dolci nodi gli avvolgea,
e 'l vago lume oltra misura ardea
4   di quei begli occhi ch'or ne son sí scarsi;

e 'l viso di pietosi color farsi,
non so se vero o falso, mi parea:
i' che l'esca amorosa al petto avea,
8   qual meraviglia se di subito arsi?

Non era l'andar suo cosa mortale,
ma d'angelica forma, e le parole
11   sonavan altro che pur voce umana;

uno spirto celeste, un vivo sole
fu quel ch' i' vidi; e se non fosse or tale,
14   piaga per allentar d'arco non sana.

17 (CXXII)

Dicessette anni ha già rivolto il cielo
poi che 'mprima arsi, e già mai non mi spensi,
ma quando avven ch' al mio stato ripensi
4 sento nel mezzo de le fiamme un gelo.

Vero è 'l proverbio, ch' altri cangia il pelo
anzi che 'l vezzo, e, per lentar i sensi,
gli umani affetti non son meno intensi;
8 ciò ne fa l'ombra ria del grave velo.

Oi me lasso! e quando fia quel giorno
che mirando il fuggir de gli anni miei
11 esca del foco e di sí lunghe pene?

Vedrò mai il dí che pur quant' io vorrei
quell' aria dolce del bel viso adorno
14 piaccia a quest' occhi, e quanto si convene?

18 (CXXIII)

Quel vago impallidir che 'l dolce riso
d' un' amorosa nebbia ricoperse,
con tanta maiestade al cor s' offerse
4   che li si fece incontr' a mezzo 'l viso.

Conobbi allor sí come in paradiso
vede l' un l' altro; in tal guisa s' aperse
quel pietoso penser, ch' altri non scerse,
8   ma vidil io, ch' altrove non m' affiso.

Ogni angelica vista, ogni atto umile
che già mai in donna ov' amor fosse apparve,
11   fora uno sdegno a lato a quel ch' io dico.

Chinava a terra il bel guardo gentile,
e tacendo dicea, come a me parve:
14   «Chi m' allontana il mio fedele amico?»

19 (CXXV)

Se 'l pensier che mi strugge,
com' è pungente e saldo,
cosí vestisse d' un color conforme,
forse tal m' arde e fugge,
ch' avria parte del caldo,
6   e desteriasi amor là dov' or dorme;
men solitarie l' orme
foran de' miei pie' lassi
per campagne e per colli,
men gli occhi ad ogn' or molli,
11   ardendo lei che come un ghiaccio stassi
e non lascia in me dramma
13   che non sia foco e fiamma.

Però ch' amor mi sforza
e di saver mi spoglia,
parlo in rime aspre e di dolcezza ignude;
ma non sempre a la scorza
ramo, né in fior né 'n foglia,
19   mostra di for sua natural vertude.
Miri ciò che 'l cor chiude
amor e que' begli occhi
ove si siede a l' ombra.
Se 'l dolor che si sgombra
24   avven che 'n pianto o in lamentar trabocchi,
l' un a me noce, e l'altro
26   altrui, ch' io non lo scaltro.

Dolci rime leggiadre,
che nel primiero assalto
d'amor usai, quand' io non ebbi altr' arme,
chi verrà mai che squadre
questo mio cor di smalto,
32   ch' almen, com' io solea, possa sfogarme?

ch' aver dentro a lui parme
un che madonna sempre
depinge e de lei parla:
a voler poi ritrarla
37   per me non basto, e par ch' io me ne stempre;
lasso, cosí m' è scorso
39   lo mio dolce soccorso!

Come fanciul ch' a pena
volge la lingua e snoda,
che dir non sa, ma 'l piú tacer gli è noia,
cosí 'l desir mi mena
a dire, e vo' che m' oda
45   la dolce mia nemica anzi ch' io moia.
Se forse ogni sua gioia
nel suo bel viso è solo,
e di tutt' altro è schiva,
odil tu, verde riva,
50   e presta a' miei sospir sí largo volo
che sempre si ridica
52   come tu m' eri amica.

Ben sai che sí bel piede
non toccò terra unquanco
come quel dí che già segnata fosti,
onde 'l cor lasso riede
col tormentoso fianco
58   a partir teco i lor pensier nascosti.
Cosí avestú riposti
de' be' vestigi sparsi
ancor tra' fiori e l' erba,
che la mia vita acerba
63   lagrimando trovasse ove acquetarsi!
ma come po s' appaga
65   l' alma dubbiosa e vaga.

Ovunque gli occhi volgo
trovo un dolce sereno
pensando: «Qui percosse il vago lume.»
Qualunque erba o fior colgo,
credo che nel terreno
71 aggia radice, ov' ella ebbe in costume
gir fra le piagge e 'l fiume,
e talor farsi un seggio
fresco, fiorito e verde.
Cosí nulla sen perde,
76 e piú certezza averne fora il peggio.
Spirto beato, quale
78 se', quando altrui fai tale?

O poverella mia, come se' rozza!
credo che tel conoschi:
81 rimanti in questi boschi.

20 (CXXVI)

Chiare, fresche e dolci acque,
ove le belle membra
pose colei che sola a me par donna;
gentil ramo, ove piacque
(con sospir mi rimembra)
6   a lei di fare al bel fianco colonna;
erba e fior, che la gonna
leggiadra ricoverse
co l' angelico seno;
aere sacro sereno,
11   ove amor co' begli occhi il cor m' aperse:
date udienzia insieme
13   a le dolenti mie parole estreme.

S' egli è pur mio destino,
e 'l cielo in ciò s' adopra,
ch' amor quest' occhi lagrimando chiuda,
qualche grazia il meschino
corpo fra voi ricopra,
19   e torni l' alma al proprio albergo ignuda;
la morte fia men cruda
se questa spene porto
a quel dubbioso passo;
ché lo spirito lasso
24   non poria mai in piú riposato porto
né in piú tranquilla fossa
26   fuggir la carne travagliata e l'ossa.

Tempo verrà ancor forse
ch' a l' usato soggiorno
torni la fera bella e mansueta,
e là 'v' ella mi scorse
nel benedetto giorno
32   volga la vista disiosa e lieta,
cercandomi; ed o pièta!

già terra infra le pietre
vedendo, amor l' ispiri
in guisa che sospiri
37　　sí dolcemente che mercé m' impetre,
e faccia forza al cielo
39　　asciugandosi gli occhi col bel velo.

Da' be' rami scendea,
dolce ne la memoria,
una pioggia di fior sovra 'l suo grembo,
ed ella si sedea
umile in tanta gloria,
45　　coverta già de l' amoroso nembo;
qual fior cadea sul lembo;
qual su le treccie bionde,
ch' oro forbito e perle
eran quel dí a vederle;
50　　qual si posava in terra e qual su l' onde;
qual con un vago errore
52　　girando parea dir: «Qui regna amore».

Quante volte diss' io
allor pien di spavento:
«Costei per fermo nacque in paradiso!»
Cosí carco d' oblio
il divin portamento
58　　e 'l volto e le parole e 'l dolce riso
m' aveano, e sí diviso
da l' imagine vera,
ch' i' dicea sospirando:
«Qui come venn' io o quando?»
63　　credendo esser in ciel, non là dov' era.
Da indi in qua mi piace
65　　quest'erba sí, ch' altrove non ho pace.

Se tu avessi ornamenti quant' hai voglia,
poresti arditamente
68　　uscir del bosco e gir infra la gente.

21 (CXXVIII)

Italia mia, benché 'l parlar sia indarno
a le piaghe mortali
che nel bel corpo tuo sí spesse veggio,
piacemi almen ch' e' miei sospir sian quali
spera 'l Tevero, e l' Arno
6   e 'l Po, dove doglioso e grave or seggio.
Rettor del cielo, io cheggio
che la pietà che ti condusse in terra
ti volga al tuo diletto almo paese:
vedi, segnor cortese,
11   di che lievi cagion che crudel guerra;
e i cor, che 'ndura e serra
Marte superbo e fero,
apri tu, Padre, e 'ntenerisci e snoda;
ivi fa che 'l tuo vero,
16   qual io mi sia, per la mia lingua s' oda.

Voi cui fortuna ha posto in mano il freno
de le belle contrade,
di che nulla pietà par che vi stringa,
che fan qui tante pellegrine spade?
perché 'l verde terreno
22   del barbarico sangue si depinga?
Vano error vi lusinga;
poco vedete e parvi veder molto,
ché 'n cor venale amor cercate o fede:
qual piú gente possede,
27   colui è piú da' suoi nemici avvolto.
O diluvio raccolto
di che deserti strani
per inondar i nostri dolci campi!
Se da le proprie mani
32   questo n' avvene, or chi fia che ne scampi?

Ben provvide natura al nostro stato,
quando de l' Alpi schermo
pose fra noi e la tedesca rabbia;
ma 'l desir cieco e 'ncontr' al suo ben fermo
s' è poi tanto ingegnato,
38   ch' al corpo sano ha procurato scabbia.
Or dentro ad una gabbia
fiere selvagge e mansuete gregge
s'annidan sí che sempre il miglior geme;
et è questo del seme,
43   per piú dolor, del popol senza legge,
al qual, come si legge,
Mario aperse sí 'l fianco
che memoria de l' opra anco non langue,
quando, assetato e stanco,
48   non piú bevve del fiume acqua che sangue.

Cesare taccio, che per ogni piaggia
fece l' erbe sanguigne
di lor vene ove 'l nostro ferro mise.
Or par, non so per che stelle maligne,
che 'l cielo in odio n' aggia:
54   vostra mercé, cui tanto si commise.
Vostre voglie divise
guastan del mondo la piú bella parte.
Qual colpa, qual giudicio o qual destino
fastidire il vicino
59   povero, e le fortune afflitte e sparte
perseguire, e 'n disparte
cercar gente e gradire
che sparga 'l sangue e venda l' alma a prezzo?
Io parlo per ver dire,
64   non per odio d' altrui né per disprezzo.

Né v' accorgete ancor per tante prove
del bavarico inganno

ch' alzando il dito colla morte scherza?
Peggio è lo strazio, al mio parer, che 'l danno.
Ma 'l vostro sangue piove
70   piú largamente: ch' altr' ira vi sferza.
Da la mattina a terza
di voi pensate, e vederete come
tien caro altrui chi tien sé cosí vile.
Latin sangue gentile,
75   sgombra da te queste dannose some;
non far idolo un nome
vano, senza soggetto;
ché 'l furor de lassú, gente ritrosa,
vincerne d' intelletto,
80   peccato è nostro e non natural cosa.

Non è questo 'l terren ch' i' toccai pria?
non è questo il mio nido,
ove nudrito fui sí dolcemente?
non è questa la patria in ch' io mi fido,
madre benigna e pia,
86   che copre l' un e l'altro mio parente?
Per Dio, questo la mente
talor vi mova, e con pietà guardate
le lagrime del popol doloroso,
che sol da voi riposo
91   dopo Dio spera; e pur che voi mostriate
segno alcun di pietate,
vertú contra furore
prenderà l' arme e fia 'l combatter corto:
ché l'antico valore
96   ne l' italici cor non è ancor morto.

Signor, mirate come 'l tempo vola,
e sí come la vita
fugge e la morte n' è sovra le spalle.
Voi siete or qui, pensate a la partita:
ché l' alma ignuda e sola

102   conven ch' arrive a quel dubbioso calle.
               Al passar questa valle
               piacciavi porre giú l' odio e lo sdegno,
               venti contrari a la vita serena,
               e quel che 'n altrui pena
107   tempo si spende, in qualche atto piú degno
               o di mano o d' ingegno,
               in qualche bella lode,
               in qualche onesto studio si converta;
               cosí qua giú si gode
112   e la strada del ciel si trova aperta.

               Canzone, io t' ammonisco
               che tua ragion cortesemente dica,
               perché fra gente altera ir ti convene,
               e le voglie son piene
               già de l' usanza pessima et antica,
118   del ver sempre nemica.
               Proverai tua ventura
               fra' magnanimi pochi a chi 'l ben piace;
               di' lor: «Chi m' assicura?
122   I' vo gridando: Pace, pace, pace».

22 (CXXIX)

Di pensier in pensier, di monte in monte
mi guida amor: ch' ogni segnato calle
provo contrario a la tranquilla vita.
Se 'n solitaria piaggia, rivo o fonte,
se 'nfra duo poggi siede ombrosa valle,
6   ivi s' acqueta l' alma sbigottita;
e come amor l' envita,
or ride or piange, or teme or s' assecura;
e 'l volto che lei segue ov' ella il mena
si turba e rasserena,
11   et in un esser picciol tempo dura;
onde a la vista uom di tal vita esperto
13   diria: «Questo arde, e di suo stato è incerto».

Per alti monti e per selve aspre trovo
qualche riposo: ogni abitato loco
è nemico mortal de gli occhi miei.
A ciascun passo nasce un penser novo
de la mia donna, che sovente in gioco
19   gira 'l tormento ch' i' porto per lei;
et a pena vorrei
cangiar questo mio viver dolce amaro,
ch' i' dico: «Forse ancor ti serva amore
ad un tempo migliore;
24   forse a te stesso vile, altrui se' caro»;
et in questa trapasso sospirando;
26   «Or porrebbe esser vero? or come? or quando?»

Ove porge ombra un pino alto od un colle,
talor m' arresto, e pur nel primo sasso
disegno co la mente il suo bel viso.
Poi ch' a me torno, trovo il petto molle
de la pietate, et allor dico: «Ahi lasso,
32   dove se' giunto, et onde se' diviso!»

Ma mentre tener fiso
posso al primo pensier la mente vaga,
e mirar lei et obliar me stesso,
sento amor sí da presso
37   che del suo proprio error l' alma s' appaga:
in tante parti e sí bella la veggio,
39   che se l' error durasse altro non cheggio.

I' l' ho piú volte (or chi fia che m' il creda?)
ne l' acqua chiara e sopra l'erba verde
veduto viva, e nel troncon d' un faggio,
e 'n bianca nube, sí fatta che Leda
avria ben detto che sua figlia perde,
45   come stella che 'l sol copre col raggio;
e quanto in piú selvaggio
loco mi trovo e 'n piú deserto lido,
tanto piú bella il mio pensier l' adombra.
Poi quando il vero sgombra
50   quel dolce error, pur lí medesmo assido
me freddo, pietra morta in pietra viva,
52   in guisa d' uom che pensi e pianga e scriva.

Ove d'altra montagna ombra non tocchi,
verso 'l maggiore e 'l piú espedito giogo
tirar mi suol un desiderio intenso.
Indi i miei danni a misurar con gli occhi
comincio e 'ntanto lagrimando sfogo
58   di dolorosa nebbia il cor condenso,
allor ch' i' miro e penso
quanta aria dal bel viso mi diparte,
che sempre m' è sí presso e sí lontano;
poscia fra me pian piano:
63   «Che sai tu, lasso? forse in quella parte
or di tua lontananza si sospira»;
65   et in questo penser l'alma respira.

Canzone, oltra quell'alpe,
là dove il ciel è piú sereno e lieto,
mi rivedrai sovr'un ruscel corrente
ove l'aura si sente
70   d'un fresco et odorifero laureto:
ivi è 'l mio cor e quella che 'l m' invola;
72   qui veder pòi l' imagine mia sola.

23 (CXXXII)

S'amor non è, che dunque è quel ch' io sento?
ma s'egli è amor, per Dio, che cosa e quale?
se bona, ond' è l'effetto aspro mortale?
4   se ria, ond' è sí dolce ogni tormento?

S' a mia voglia ardo, ond' è 'l pianto e lamento?
s' a mal mio grado, il lamentar che vale?
O viva morte, o dilettoso male,
8   come puoi tanto in me, s' io nol consento?

E s' io 'l consento, a gran torto mi doglio.
Fra sí contrari venti in frale barca
11   mi trovo in alto mar senza governo,

sí lieve di saver, d'error sí carca,
ch' i' medesmo non so quel ch' io mi voglio,
14   e tremo a mezza state, ardendo il verno.

24 (CXXXVI)

Fiamma dal ciel su le tue treccie piova,
malvagia, che dal fiume e da le ghiande,
per l' altrui impoverir, se' ricca e grande,
4   poi che di mal oprar tanto ti giova;

nido di tradimenti, in cui si cova
quanto mal per lo mondo oggi si spande:
de vin serva, di letti e di vivande,
8   in cui lussuria fa l' ultima prova.

Per le camere tue fanciulle e vecchi
vanno trescando, e Belzebub in mezzo
11   co' mantici e col foco e co li specchi.

Già non fostú nudrita in piume al rezzo,
ma nuda al vento e scalza fra gli stecchi:
14   or vivi sí ch' a Dio ne venga il lezzo.

25 (CLIX)

In qual parte del ciel, in quale idea
era l'esempio onde natura tolse
quel bel viso leggiadro, in ch' ella volse
4   mostrar qua giú quanto lassú potea?

Qual ninfa in fonti, in selve mai qual dea
chiome d'oro sí fino a l'aura sciolse?
quando un cor tante in sé vertuti accolse?
8   benché la somma è di mia morte rea.

Per divina bellezza indarno mira
chi gli occhi de costei già mai non vide,
11   come soavemente ella gli gira;

non sa come amor sana e come ancide
chi non sa come dolce ella sospira
14   e come dolce parla e dolce ride.

26 (CLX)

Amor ed io sí pien di meraviglia,
come chi mai cosa incredibil vide,
miriam costei quand' ella parla o ride,
4   che sol se stessa e nulla altra simiglia.

Dal bel seren de le tranquille ciglia
sfavillan sí le mie due stelle fide
ch' altro lume non è ch'infiammi e guide
8   chi d'amar altamente si consiglia.

Qual miracolo è quel, quando tra l'erba
quasi un fior siede, ovver quand'ella preme
11   col suo candido seno un verde cespo!

Qual dolcezza è ne la stagione acerba
vederla ir sola coi pensier suoi inseme,
14   tessendo un cerchio a l'oro terso e crespo!

27 (CLXIV)

Or che 'l ciel e la terra e 'l vento tace,
e le fere e gli augelli il sonno affrena,
notte il carro stellato in giro mena,
4   e nel suo letto il mar senz' onda giace,

vegghio, penso, ardo, piango, e chi mi sface
sempre m' è inanzi per mia dolce pena:
guerra è 'l mio stato, d' ira e di duol piena,
8   e sol di lei pensando ho qualche pace.

Cosí sol d'una chiara fonte viva
move 'l dolce e l'amaro ond' io mi pasco;
11   una man sola mi risana e punge;

e perché 'l mio martir non giunga a riva,
mille volte il dí moro e mille nasco:
14   tanto da la salute mia son lunge.

28 (CLXX)

Piú volte già dal bel sembiante umano
ho preso ardir co le mie fide scorte
d'assalir con parole oneste accorte
4   la mia nemica in atto umile e piano.

Fanno poi gli occhi suoi mio penser vano,
per ch' ogni mia fortuna, ogni mia sorte,
mio ben, mio male, e mia vita e mia morte
8   quei che solo il po far l' ha posto in mano.

Ond' io non pote' mai formar parola
ch' altro che da me stesso fosse intesa:
11   cosí m' ha fatto amor tremante e fioco!

E veggi' or ben che caritate accesa
lega la lingua altrui, gli spirti invola:
14   chi po dir com' egli arde è 'n picciol foco.

29 (CLXXXIII)

Se 'l dolce sguardo di costei m' ancide,
e le soavi parolette accorte,
e s' amor sopra me la fa sí forte,
4   sol quando parla, ovver quando sorride,

lasso! che fia, se forse ella divide,
o per mia colpa o per malvagia sorte,
gli occhi suoi da mercé, sí che di morte
8   là dove or m' assicura, allor mi sfide?

Però s' i' tremo e vo col cor gelato,
qualor veggio cangiata sua figura,
11   questo temer d' antiche prove è nato.

Femina è cosa mobil per natura;
ond' io so ben ch' un amoroso stato
14   in cor di donna picciol tempo dura.

30 (CLXXXIX)

Passa la nave mia, colma d' oblio,
per aspro mare, a mezza notte, il verno,
enfra Scilla e Caribdi; et al governo
4   siede 'l signore, anzi 'l nimico mio;

a ciascun remo un penser pronto e rio
che la tempesta e 'l fin par ch'abbi a scherno;
la vela rompe un vento umido, eterno
8   di sospir, di speranze e di desio;

pioggia di lagrimar, nebbia di sdegni
bagna e rallenta le già stanche sarte,
11   che son d' error con ignoranzia attorto.

Celansi i duo mei dolci usati segni;
morta fra l' onde è la ragion e l' arte:
14   tal ch' i' 'ncomincio a desperar del porto.

3I (CXCII)

Stiamo, amor, a veder la gloria nostra:
cose sopra natura altere e nove.
Vedi ben quanta in lei dolcezza piove,
4   vedi lume che 'l cielo in terra mostra!

Vedi quant' arte dora e 'mperla e 'nostra
l' abito eletto e mai non visto altrove,
che dolcemente i piedi e gli occhi move
8   per questa di bei colli ombrosa chiostra!

L'erbetta verde e i fior di color mille
sparsi sotto quell'elce antiqua e negra,
11   pregan pur che 'l bel pè li prema o tocchi;

e 'l ciel di vaghe e lucide faville
s' accende intorno, e 'n vista si rallegra
14   d' esser fatto seren da sí belli occhi.

32 (CCVIII)

Rapido fiume, che d' alpestra vena
rodendo intorno, onde 'l tuo nome prendi,
notte e dí meco disioso scendi
4   ov'amor me, te sol natura mena,

vattene innanzi: il tuo corso non frena
né stanchezza né sonno, e pria che rendi
suo dritto al mar, fiso u' si mostri attendi
8   l' erba piú verde e l' aria piú serena.

Ivi è quel nostro vivo e dolce sole
ch' adorna e 'nfiora la tua riva manca;
11   forse (o che spero?) el mio tardar le dole.

Basciale 'l piede o la man bella e bianca;
dille, e 'l basciar sie 'n vece di parole:
14   «Lo spirto è pronto, ma la carne è stanca.»

33 (CCXIX)

Il cantar novo e 'l pianger delli augelli
in sul dí fanno retentir le valli,
e 'l mormorar de' liquidi cristalli
4   giú per lucidi freschi rivi e snelli.

Quella c'ha neve il volto, oro i capelli,
nel cui amor non fur mai inganni né falli,
destami al suon delli amorosi balli,
8   pettinando al suo vecchio i bianchi velli.

Cosí mi sveglio a salutar l' aurora
e 'l sol ch' è seco, e piú l' altro ond' io fui
11   ne' primi anni abbagliato e son ancora;

i' gli ho veduti alcun giorno ambedui
levarsi inseme, e 'n un punto e 'n un' ora
14   quel far le stelle, e questo sparir lui.

34 (CCXXVI)

Passer mai solitario in alcun tetto
non fu quant'io, né fera in alcun bosco,
ch' i' non veggio 'l bel viso, e non conosco
4   altro sol, né quest' occhi hann' altro obietto.

Lagrimar sempre è 'l mio sommo diletto,
il rider doglia, il cibo assenzio e tosco,
la notte affanno, e 'l ciel seren m' è fosco,
8   e duro campo di battaglia il letto.

Il sonno è veramente, qual uom dice,
parente de la morte, e 'l cor sottragge
11   a quel dolce penser che 'n vita il tene.

Solo al mondo paese almo felice,
verdi rive fiorite, ombrose piagge,
14   voi possedete, et io piango, il mio bene.

35 (CCXXXIV)

O cameretta, che già fosti un porto
a le gravi tempeste mie diurne,
fonte se' or di lagrime notturne,
4   che 'l dí celate per vergogna porto.

O letticciuol, che requie eri e conforto
in tanti affanni, di che dogliose urne
ti bagna amor con quelle mani eburne,
8   solo ver me crudeli a sí gran torto.

Né pur il mio secreto e 'l mio riposo
fuggo, ma piú me stesso e 'l mio pensero,
11   che, seguendol, talor levommi a volo;

e 'l vulgo, a me nemico et odioso
(chi 'l pensò mai?) per mio refugio chero:
14   tal paura ho di ritrovarmi solo.

36 (CCXXXVIII)

Real natura, angelico intelletto,
chiara alma, pronta vista, occhio cerviero,
providenzia veloce, alto pensero
4 e veramente degno di quel petto:

sendo di donne un bel numero eletto
per adornar il dí festo et altero,
subito scorse il buon giudicio intero
8 fra tanti e sí bei volti il piú perfetto.

L' altre, maggior di tempo o di fortuna,
trarsi in disparte comandò con mano
11 e caramente accolse a sé quell' una;

li occhi e la fronte con sembiante umano
basciolle sí che rallegrò ciascuna:
14 me empié d' invidia l' atto dolce e strano.

37 (CCXLV)

Due rose fresche e colte in paradiso
l' altr' ier, nascendo il dí primo di maggio,
bel dono e d' un amante antiquo e saggio
4   tra duo minori egualmente diviso,

con sí dolce parlar e con un riso
da far innamorare un uom selvaggio,
di sfavillante ed amoroso raggio
8   e l' un' e l' altro fe' cangiare il viso.

«Non vede un simil par d' amanti il sole»
dicea, ridendo e sospirando inseme;
11   e stringendo ambedue, volgeasi a torno.

Cosí partia le rose e le parole,
onde 'l cor lasso ancor s' allegra e teme:
14   o felice eloquenzia! o lieto giorno!

38 (CCL)

Solea lontana in sonno consolarme
con quella dolce angelica sua vista
madonna; or mi spaventa e mi contrista,
4   né di duol né di tema posso aitarme;

ché spesso nel suo volto veder parme
vera pietà con grave dolor mista,
et udir cose onde 'l cor fede acquista
8   che di gioia e di speme si disarme.

«Non ti soven di quella ultima sera»
dice ella «ch' i' lasciai li occhi tuoi molli,
11   e sforzata dal tempo me n' andai?

I' non tel potei dir allor, né volli;
or tel dico per cosa esperta e vera:
14   non sperar di vedermi in terra mai».

39 (CCLXIV)

I' vo pensando, e nel penser m' assale
una pietà sí forte di me stesso,
che mi conduce spesso
ad altro lagrimar ch' i' non soleva;
ché, vedendo ogni giorno il fin piú presso,
6   mille fiate ho chieste a Dio quell' ale
co le quai del mortale
carcer nostr'intelletto al ciel si leva:
ma infin a qui niente mi releva
prego o sospiro o lagrimar ch'. io faccia;
e cosí per ragion conven che sia,
12   ché chi possendo star cadde tra via
degno è che mal suo grado a terra giaccia.
Quelle pietose braccia,
in ch' io mi fido, veggio aperte ancora;
ma temenza m'accora
per gli altrui esempli, e del mio stato tremo;
18   ch' altri mi sprona e son forse a l'estremo.

L'un penser parla co la mente e dice:
«Che pur agogni? onde soccorso attendi?
misera, non intendi
con quanto tuo disnore il tempo passa?
Prendi partito accortamente, prendi,
24   e del cor tuo divelli ogni radice
del piacer, che felice
nol po mai fare, e respirar nol lassa.
Se già è gran tempo fastidita e lassa
se' di quel falso dolce fuggitivo
che 'l mondo traditor può dare altrui,
30   a che ripon piú la speranza in lui,
che d' ogni pace e di fermezza è privo?
Mentre che 'l corpo è vivo

hai tu 'l freno in bailia de' penser tuoi.
Deh stringilo or che pòi,
ché dubbioso è 'l tardar, come tu sai,
36   e 'l cominciar non fia per tempo omai.

Già sai tu ben quanta dolcezza porse
agli occhi tuoi la vista di colei,
la qual anco vorrei
ch' a nascer fosse per piú nostra pace.
Ben ti ricordi, e ricordar ten dei,
42   de l' imagine sua, quand' ella corse
al cor, là dove forse
non potea fiamma intrar per altrui face.
Ella l' accese, e se l' ardor fallace
durò molt' anni in aspettando un giorno
che per nostra salute unqua non vene,
48   or ti solleva a piú beata spene,
mirando 'l ciel che ti si volve intorno
immortal et adorno:
ché dove del mal suo qua giú sí lieta
vostra vaghezza acqueta
un mover d' occhi, un ragionar, un canto,
54   quanto fia quel piacer, se questo è tanto?»

Da l' altra parte un pensier dolce et agro
con faticosa e dilettevol salma
sedendosi entro l' alma,
preme 'l cor di desio, di speme il pasce;
che sol per fama gloriosa et alma
60   non sente quand'io agghiaccio o quand'io flagro,
s' i' son pallido o magro;
e s' io l' occido, piú forte rinasce.
Questo d' allor ch' i' m' addormiva in fasce
venuto è di dí in dí crescendo meco,
e temo ch' un sepolcro ambeduo chiuda:
66   poi che fia l' alma de le membra ignuda,
non po questo desio piú venir seco.
Ma se 'l latino e 'l greco

parlan di me dopo la morte, è un vento:
ond' io, perché pavento
adunar sempre quel ch' un' ora sgombre,
72   vorre' 'l ver abbracciar, lassando l' ombre.

Ma quell' altro voler di ch' i' son pieno
quanti press' a lui nascon par ch' adugge,
e parte il tempo fugge
ché, scrivendo d' altrui, di me non calme;
e 'l lume de' begli occhi, che mi strugge
78   soavemente al suo caldo sereno,
mi ritien con un freno
contra cui nullo ingegno o forza valme.
Che giova dunque perché tutta spalme
la mia barchetta, poi che 'nfra li scogli
è ritenuta ancor da ta' duo nodi?
84   Tu che dagli altri che 'n diversi modi
legano 'l mondo in tutto mi disciogli,
Signor mio, ché non togli
omai dal volto mio questa vergogna?
Ché 'n guisa d'uom che sogna,
aver la morte inanzi gli occhi parme,
90   e vorrei far difesa e non ho l' arme.

Quel ch' i' fo, veggio, e non m' inganna il vero
mal conosciuto, anzi mi sforza amore,
che la strada d' onore
mai nol lassa seguir chi troppo il crede;
e sento ad ora ad or venirmi al core
96   un leggiadro disdegno, aspro e severo,
ch' ogni occulto pensero
tira in mezzo la fronte, ov' altri 'l vede;
ché mortal cosa amar con tanta fede,
quanto a Dio sol per debito convensi,
piú si disdice a chi piú pregio brama.
102   E questo ad alta voce anco richiama
la ragione sviata dietro ai sensi:
ma perch' ell' oda e pensi

tornare, il mal costume oltre la spigne
et agli occhi depigne
quella che sol per farmi morir nacque,
108 perch' a me troppo et a se stessa piacque.

Né so che spazio mi si desse il cielo
quando novellamente io venni in terra
a soffrir l' aspra guerra
che 'ncontra me medesmo seppi ordire,
né posso il giorno che la vita serra,
114 antiveder per lo corporeo velo;
ma variarsi il pelo
veggio e dentro cangiarsi ogni desire.
Or ch' i' mi credo al tempo del partire
esser vicino o non molto da lunge,
come chi 'l perder face accorto e saggio,
120 vo ripensando ov' io lassai 'l viaggio
da la man destra, ch' a buon porto aggiunge:
e da l' un lato punge
vergogna e duol, che 'ndietro mi rivolve;
dall' altro non m' assolve
un piacer per usanza in me sí forte,
126 ch' a patteggiar n' ardisce co la morte.

Canzon, qui sono, ed ho 'l cor via piú freddo
de la paura che gelata neve,
sentendomi perir senz' alcun dubbio,
ché pur deliberando ho volto al subbio
gran parte omai de la mia tela breve;
132 né mai peso fu greve
quanto quel ch' i' sostengo in tale stato:
ché co la morte a lato
cerco del viver mio novo consiglio;
136 e veggio 'l meglio et al peggior m' appiglio.

40 (CCLXVIII)

Che debb' io far? che mi consigli, amore?
Tempo è ben di morire
ed ho tardato più ch' i' non vorrei:
madonna è morta ed ha seco il mio core,
e volendol seguire
6   interromper conven quest' anni rei,
perché mai veder lei
di qua non spero, e l' aspettar m' è noia:
poscia ch' ogni mia gioia
per lo suo dipartire in pianto è volta,
11   ogni dolcezza de mia vita è tolta.

Amor, tu 'l senti, ond' io teco mi doglio,
quant' è 'l danno aspro e grave,
e so che del mio mal ti pesa e dole:
anzi del nostro, perch' ad uno scoglio
avem rotto la nave
17   ed in un punto n' è scurato il sole.
Qual ingegno a parole
poria aguagliare il mio doglioso stato?
Ahi! orbo mondo ingrato,
gran cagion hai di dover pianger meco,
22   ché quel bel ch' era in te perduto hai seco.

Caduta è la tua gloria, e tu nol vedi,
né degno eri, mentr'ella
visse qua giú, d' aver sua conoscenza,
né d' esser tocco da' suoi santi piedi,
perché cosa sí bella
28   devea 'l ciel adornar di sua presenza.
Ma io, lasso, che senza
lei né la vita mortal né me stesso amo,
piangendo la richiamo:
questo m' avanza di cotanta spene,
33   e questo solo ancor qui mi mantene.

Oimè, terra è fatto il suo bel viso,
che solea far del cielo
e del ben di lassú fede fra noi;
l'invisibil sua forma è in paradiso,
disciolta di quel velo
39   che qui fece ombra al fior degli anni suoi,
per rivestirsen poi
un' altra volta e mai piú non spogliarsi,
quando alma e bella farsi
tanto piú la vedrem quanto piú vale
44   sempiterna bellezza che mortale.

Piú che mai bella e piú leggiadra donna
tornami inanzi, come
là dove piú gradir sua vista sente;
questa è del viver mio l' una colonna,
l' altra è 'l suo chiaro nome
50   che sona nel mio cor sí dolcemente.
Ma, tornandomi a mente
che pur morta è la mia speranza, viva
allor ch'ella fioriva,
sa ben amor qual io divento e, spero,
55   vedel colei ch'è or sí presso al vero.

Donne, voi che miraste sua beltate
e l' angelica vita,
con quel celeste portamento in terra,
di me vi doglia e vincavi pietate:
non di lei, ch' è salita
61   a tanta pace e m' ha lassato in guerra,
tal che, s' altri mi serra
lungo tempo il cammin da seguitarla,
quel ch' amor meco parla
sol mi riten ch' io non recida il nodo,
66   ma e' ragiona dentro in cotal modo:

«Pon freno al gran dolor che ti trasporta:
ché per soverchie voglie

si perde 'l cielo ove 'l tuo core aspira,
dove è viva colei ch' altrui par morta,
e di sue belle spoglie
72   seco sorride e sol di te sospira;
e sua fama che spira
in molte parti ancor per la tua lingua,
prega che non estingua,
anzi la voce al suo nome rischiari,
77   se gli occhi suoi ti fur dolci né cari».

Fuggi 'l sereno e 'l verde,
non t' appressare ove sia riso o canto,
canzon mia no, ma pianto:
non fa per te di star fra gente allegra,
82   vedova, sconsolata, in veste negra.

4I (CCLXXII)

La vita fugge e non s' arresta un' ora,
e la morte vien dietro a gran giornate,
e le cose presenti e le passate
4   mi danno guerra, e le future ancora;

e 'l rimembrare e l' aspettar m' accora
or quinci or quindi, sí che 'n veritate,
se non ch' i' ho di me stesso pietate,
8   i' sarei già di questi pensier fora.

Tornami avanti s' alcun dolce mai
ebbe 'l cor tristo, e poi da l' altra parte
11   veggio al mio navigar turbati i venti;

veggio fortuna in porto, e stanco omai
il mio nocchier, e rotte arbore e sarte,
14   e i lumi bei che mirar soglio, spenti.

42 (CCLXXIX)

Se lamentar augelli, o verdi fronde
mover soavemente a l' aura estiva,
o roco mormorar di lucide onde
4   s' ode d' una fiorita e fresca riva,

là 'v' io seggia d' amor pensoso e scriva,
lei che 'l ciel ne mostrò, terra n' asconde,
veggio et odo et intendo, ch' ancor viva
8   di sí lontano a' sospir miei risponde:

«Deh perché inanzi 'l tempo ti consume?»
mi dice con pietate «a che pur versi
11   degli occhi tristi un doloroso fiume?

Di me non pianger tu, ché ' miei dí fersi
morendo eterni, e ne l' interno lume,
14   quando mostrai de chiuder, gli occhi apersi».

43 (CCLXXX)

Mai non fui in parte ove sí chiar vedessi
quel che veder vorrei, poi ch' io nol vidi,
né dove in tanta libertà mi stessi
né 'mpiessi il ciel de sí amorosi stridi;

né già mai vidi valle aver sí spessi
luoghi da sospirar riposti e fidi;
né credo già ch'amore in Cipro avessi
o in altra riva sí soavi nidi.

L' acque parlan d' amore e l'òra e i rami
e gli augelletti e i pesci e i fiori e l' erba,
tutti inseme pregando ch' i' sempre ami.

Ma tu, ben nata, che dal ciel mi chiami,
per la memoria di tua morte acerba
preghi ch' i' sprezzi 'l mondo e i suoi dolci ami.

44 (CCLXXXVII)

Sennuccio mio, benché doglioso e solo
m' abbi lasciato, i' pur mi riconforto,
perché del corpo, ov' eri preso e morto,
4　　alteramente se' levato a volo.

Or vedi inseme l' un e l' altro polo,
le stelle vaghe e lor viaggio torto,
e vedi il veder nostro quanto è corto:
8　　onde col tuo gioir tempro 'l mio duolo.

Ma ben ti prego che 'n la terza spera
Guitton saluti e messer Cino e Dante,
11　　Franceschin nostro e tutta quella schiera;

a la mia donna puoi ben dire in quante
lagrime io vivo e son fatt' una fera,
14　　membrando il suo bel viso e l' opre sante.

45 (CCLXXXIX)

L'alma mia fiamma oltra le belle bella,
ch' ebbe qui 'l ciel sí amico e sí cortese,
anzi tempo per me nel suo paese
4   è ritornata et a la par sua stella.

Or comincio a svegliarmi, e veggio ch' ella
per lo migliore al mio desir contese,
e quelle voglie giovenili accese
8   temprò con una vista dolce e fella;

lei ne ringrazio e 'l suo alto consiglio,
che, col bel viso e co' soavi sdegni,
11   fecemi, ardendo, pensar mia salute.

O leggiadre arti e lor effetti degni,
l' un co la lingua oprar, l' altra col ciglio,
14   io gloria in lei, ed ella in me virtute!

46 (CCXCII)

Gli occhi di ch' iò parlai sí caldamente,
e le braccia e le mani e i piedi e 'l viso,
che m' avean sí da me stesso diviso
4   e fatto singular da l' altra gente;

le crespe chiome d' or puro lucente
e 'l lampeggiar de l' angelico riso,
che solean fare in terra un paradiso,
8   poca polvere son che nulla sente;

et io pur vivo, onde mi doglio e sdegno,
rimaso senza 'l lume ch' amai tanto,
11   in gran fortuna e 'n disarmato legno.

Or sia qui fine al mio amoroso canto:
secca è la vena de l' usato ingegno
14   e la cetera mia rivolta in pianto.

47 (CCCI)

Valle, che de' lamenti miei se' piena,
fiume, che spesso del mio pianger cresci,
fere selvestre, vaghi augelli e pesci,
4   che l' una e l' altra verde riva affrena;

aria, de' miei sospir calda e serena,
dolce sentier, che sí amaro riesci,
colle che mi piacesti, or mi rincresci,
8   ov'ancor per usanza amor mi mena:

ben riconosco in voi l' usate forme,
non, lasso, in me, che da sí lieta vita
11   son fatto albergo d' infinita doglia.

Quinci vedea 'l mio bene, e per queste orme
torno a vedere ond' al ciel nuda è gita,
14   lasciando in terra la sua bella spoglia.

48 (CCCII)

Levommi il mio penser in parte ov' era
quella ch' io cerco e non ritrovo in terra:
ivi, fra lor che 'l terzo cerchio serra,
4   la rividi piú bella e meno altera.

Per man mi prese e disse: «In questa spera
sarai ancor meco, se 'l desir non erra:
i' so' colei che ti die' tanta guerra
8   e compie' mia giornata inanzi sera.

Mio ben non cape in intelletto umano:
te solo aspetto, e quel che tanto amasti
11   e là giuso è rimaso, il mio bel velo».

Deh, perché tacque ed allargò la mano?
ch' al suon de' detti sí pietosi e casti
14   poco mancò ch' io non rimasi in cielo.

49 (CCCIV)

Mentre che 'l cor dagli amorosi vermi
fu consumato e 'n fiamma amorosa arse,
di vaga fera le vestigia sparse
4   cercai per poggi solitari et ermi,

ed ebbi ardir, cantando, di dolermi
d'amor, di lei che sí dura m' apparse;
ma l' ingegno e le rime erano scarse
8   in quella etate ai pensier novi e 'nfermi.

Quel foco è morto e 'l copre un picciol marmo,
che se col tempo fossi ito avanzando,
11   come già in altri, infino a la vecchiezza,

di rime armato ond' oggi mi disarmo,
con stil canuto avrei fatto, parlando,
14   romper le pietre e pianger di dolcezza.

50 (CCCX)

Zefiro torna e 'l bel tempo rimena,
e i fiori e l' erbe, sua dolce famiglia,
e garrir Progne e pianger Filomena,
4   e primavera candida e vermiglia;

ridono i prati e 'l ciel si rasserena,
Giove s' allegra di mirar sua figlia,
l' aria e l' acqua e la terra è d' amor piena,
8   ogni animal d' amar si riconsiglia.

Ma per me, lasso, tornano i piú gravi
sospiri, che del cor profondo tragge
11   quella ch' al ciel se ne portò le chiavi;

e cantar augelletti e fiorir piagge
e 'n belle donne oneste atti soavi
14   sono un deserto e fere aspre e selvagge.

5I (CCCXI)

Quel rosignuol che sí soave piagne,
forse suoi figli o sua cara consorte,
di dolcezza empie il cielo e le campagne
con tante note sí pietose e scorte,

e tutta notte par che m' accompagne
e mi rammente la mia dura sorte,
ch' altri che me non ho di chi mi lagne,
ché 'n dee non credev' io regnasse morte.

O che lieve è ingannar chi s' assecura!
Que' duo bei lumi assai piú che 'l sol chiari
chi pensò mai veder far terra oscura?

Or cognosco io che mia fera ventura
vuol che vivendo e lagrimando impari
come nulla qua giú diletta e dura!

52 (CCCXV)

Tutta la mia fiorita e verde etade
passava, e 'ntepidir sentia già 'l foco
ch' arse il mio core, ed era giunto al loco
4   ove scende la vita ch' al fin cade;

già incominciava a prender securtade
la mia cara nemica a poco a poco
de' suoi sospetti, e rivolgeva in gioco
8   mie pene acerbe sua dolce onestade;

presso era 'l tempo dove amor si scontra
con castitate, ed agli amanti è dato
11   sedersi inseme e dir che lor incontra.

Morte ebbe invidia al mio felice stato,
anzi a la speme, e feglisi a l' incontra
14   a mezza via, come nemico armato.

53 (CCCXX)

Sento l' aura mia antica, e i dolci colli
veggio apparire onde 'l bel lume nacque,
che tenne gli occhi mei, mentr' al ciel piacque,
4   bramosi e lieti, or li ten tristi e molli.

O caduche speranze, o penser folli!
Vedove l' erbe e torbide son l' acque,
e voto e freddo 'l nido in ch' ella giacque,
8   nel qual io vivo e morto giacer volli,

sperando alfin da le soavi piante
e da' belli occhi suoi, che 'l cor m' hann' arso,
11   riposo alcun de le fatiche tante.

Ho servito a signor crudele e scarso:
ch' arsi quanto 'l mio foco ebbi davante,
14   or vo piangendo il suo cenere sparso.

54 (CCCXLVI)

Li angeli eletti e l'anime beate,
cittadine del cielo, il primo giorno
che madonna passò, le fur intorno
4 piene di meraviglia e di pietate.

«Che luce è questa e qual nova beltate»
dicean tra lor «perch' abito sí adorno
dal mondo errante a quest' alto soggiorno
8 non salí mai in tutta questa etate?»

Ella, contenta aver cangiato albergo,
si paragona pur coi piú perfetti,
11 e parte ad or ad or si volge a tergo,

mirando s' io la seguo, e par ch' aspetti:
ond' io voglie e pensier tutti al ciel ergo,
14 perch' i' l' odo pregar pur ch' i' m' affretti.

55 (CCCLIII)

Vago augelletto, che cantando vai
o ver piangendo il tuo tempo passato,
vedendoti la notte e 'l verno a lato
4   e 'l dí dopo le spalle e i mesi gai,

se, come i tuoi gravosi affanni sai,
cosí sapessi il mio simile stato,
verresti in grembo a questo sconsolato
8   a partir seco i dolorosi guai.

I' non so se le parti sarian pari,
ché quella cui tu piangi è forse in vita,
11   di ch' a me morte e 'l ciel son tanto avari;

ma la stagion e l' ora men gradita
col membrar de' dolci anni e de li amari
14   a parlar teco con pietà m' invita.

56 (CCCLIX)

Quando il soave mio fido conforto,
per dar riposo a la mia vita stanca,
ponsi del letto in su la sponda manca
con quel suo dolce ragionare accorto,
tutto di pièta e di paura smorto,
6 dico: «Onde vien tu ora, o felice alma?»
Un ramoscel di palma
ed un di lauro trae del suo bel seno
e dice: «Dal sereno
ciel empireo e di quelle sante parti
11 mi mossi, e vengo sol per consolarti».

In atto ed in parole la ringrazio
umilemente, e poi demando: «Or donde
sai tu il mio stato?» Ed ella: «Le triste onde
del pianto di che mai tu non se' sazio,
coll'aura de' sospir, per tanto spazio
17 passano al cielo e turban la mia pace;
sí forte ti dispiace
che di questa miseria sia partita
e giunta a miglior vita?
che piacer ti devria, se tu m' amasti
22 quanto in sembianti e ne' tuoi dir mostrasti.»

Rispondo: «Io non piango altro che me stesso
che son rimaso in tenebre e 'n martire,
certo sempre del tuo al ciel salire
come di cosa ch' uom vede da presso.
Come Dio e natura avrebben messo
28 in un cor giovenil tanta vertute,
se l'eterna salute
non fusse destinata al tuo ben fare?
o de l' anime rare,

ch' altamente vivesti qui tra noi

33   e che subito al ciel volasti poi!

Ma io che debbo altro che pianger sempre,
misero e sol, che senza te son nulla?
ch' or fuss' io spento al latte ed a la culla,
per non provar de l' amorose tempre!»
Ed ella: «A che pur piangi e ti distempre?

39   Quanto era meglio alzar da terra l' ali,
e le cose mortali
e queste dolci tue fallaci ciance
librar con giusta lance,
e seguir me, s' è ver che tanto m' ami,

44   cogliendo omai qualcun di questi rami!»

«I' volea demandar» respond' io allora
«che voglion importar quelle due frondi?»
Ed ella: «Tu medesmo ti rispondi,
tu la cui penna tanto l'una onora:
palma è vittoria, ed io, giovene ancora,

50   vinsi il mondo e me stessa; il lauro segna
triunfo, ond' io son degna
mercé di quel Signor che mi diè forza.
Or tu, s' altri ti sforza,
a lui ti volgi, a lui chiedi soccorso,

55   sí che siam seco al fine del tuo corso».

«Son questi i capei biondi e l' aureo nodo»
dich'io «ch'ancor mi stringe e quei belli occhi
che fur mio sol?» «Non errar con li sciocchi,
né parlar» dice «o creder a lor modo:
spirito ignudo sono, e 'n ciel mi godo;

61   quel che tu cerchi è terra già molt' anni;
ma per trarti d' affanni
m' è dato a parer tale, ed ancor quella
sarò, piú che mai bella,
a te piú cara, sí selvaggia e pia,

66   salvando inseme tua salute e mia».

I' piango, ed ella il volto
co le sue man m' asciuga e poi sospira
dolcemente, e s' adira
con parole che i sassi romper ponno;
71   e dopo questo si parte ella e 'l sonno.

57 (CCCLX)

Quell'antiquo mio dolce empio signore
fatto citar dinanzi a la reina
che la parte divina
tien di nostra natura e 'n cima sede,
ivi, com' oro che nel foco affina,
6   mi rappresento carco di dolore,
di paura e d' orrore,
quasi uom che teme morte e ragion chiede;
e 'ncomincio: «Madonna, il manco piede
giovenetto pos' io nel costui regno,
11   ond' altro ch' ira e sdegno
non ebbi mai, e tanti e sí diversi
tormenti ivi soffersi,
ch' alfine vinta fu quell' infinita
15   mia pazienzia, e 'n odio ebbi la vita.

Cosí 'l mio tempo infin qui trapassato
è in fiamma e 'n pene, e quante utili oneste
vie sprezzai, quante feste,
per servir questo lusinghier crudele!
E qual ingegno ha sí parole preste
21   che stringer possa 'l mio infelice stato
e le mie d' esto ingrato
tante e sí gravi e sí giuste querele?
O poco mel, molto aloè con fele!
in quanto amaro ha la mia vita avvezza
26   con sua falsa dolcezza,
la qual m' attrasse a l' amorosa schiera!
Che, s' i' non m' inganno, era
disposto a sollevarmi alto da terra:
30   e' mi tolse di pace e pose in guerra.

Questi m' ha fatto men amare Dio
ch' i' non deveva e men curar me stesso:

per una donna ho messo
egualmente in non cale ogni pensero.
Di ciò m' è stato consiglier sol esso,
36   sempr' aguzzando il giovenil desio
a l' empia cote ond' io
sperai riposo al suo giogo aspro e fero.
Misero! a che quel caro ingegno altero
e l' altre doti a me date dal cielo?
41   ché vo cangiando 'l pelo,
né cangiar posso l' ostinata voglia:
cosí in tutto mi spoglia
di libertà questo crudel ch' i' accuso,
45   ch' amaro viver m' ha volto in dolce uso.

Cercar m' ha fatto deserti paesi,
fiere e ladri rapaci, ispidi dumi,
dure genti e costumi
ed ogni error che ' pellegrini intrica;
monti, valli, paludi e mari e fiumi,
51   mille lacciuoli in ogni parte tesi,
e 'l verno in strani mesi
con pericol presente e con fatica;
né costui né quell' altra mia nemica,
ch' i' fuggia, mi lasciavan sol un punto:
56   onde, s' i' non son giunto
anzi tempo da morte acerba e dura,
pietà celeste ha cura
di mia salute, non questo tiranno,
60   che del mio duol si pasce e del mio danno.

Poi che suo fui, non ebbi ora tranquilla,
né spero aver, e le mie notti il sonno
sbandiro, e piú non ponno
per erbe o per incanti a sé ritrarlo.
Per inganni e per forza è fatto donno
66   sovra miei spirti, e non sonò poi squilla,
ov' io sia in qualche villa,

ch' i' non l' udisse. Ei sa che 'l vero parlo;
ché legno vecchio mai non rose tarlo,
come questi 'l mio core, in che s' annida
71   e di morte lo sfida;
quinci nascon le lagrime e i martiri,
le parole e i sospiri,
di ch'io mi vo stancando, e forse altrui.
75   Giudica tu, che me conosci e lui».

Il mio adversario con agre rampogne
comincia: «O donna, intendi l' altra parte,
che 'l vero, onde si parte
quest'ingrato, dirà senza defetto.
Questi in sua prima età fu dato a l' arte
81   da vender parolette, anzi menzogne:
né par che si vergogne,
tolto da quella noia al mio diletto,
lamentarsi di me, che puro e netto,
contra 'l desio che spesso il suo mal vole,
86   lui tenni, ond' or si dole,
in dolce vita ch' ei miseria chiama,
salito in qualche fama
solo per me, che 'l suo intelletto alzai
90   ov' alzato per sé non fora mai.

Ei sa che 'l grande Atride e l'alto Achille
et Anibal al terren vostro amaro
e di tutti il piú chiaro
un altro e di vertute e di fortuna,
com' a ciascun le sue stelle ordinaro,
96   lasciai cader in vil amor d' ancille:
et a costui di mille
donne elette eccellenti n' elessi una
qual non si vedrà mai sotto la luna,
benché Lucrezia ritornasse a Roma;
101   e sí dolce idioma

le diedi ed un cantar tanto soave,
che penser basso o grave
non poté mai durar dinanzi a lei:
105   questi fur con costui l' inganni mei.

Questo fu il fel, questi li sdegni e l' ire,
piú dolci assai che di null' altra il tutto.
Di bon seme mal frutto
mieto, e tal merito ha chi 'ngrato serve.
Sí l' avea sotto l' ali mie condutto,
111   ch' a donne e cavalier piacea il suo dire;
e sí alto salire
il feci, che tra' caldi ingegni ferve
il suo nome, e de' suoi detti conserve
si fanno con diletto in alcun loco;
116   ch' or saria forse un roco
mormorador di corti, un uom del vulgo:
i' l'esalto e divulgo
per quel ch' elli 'mparò ne la mia scola
120   e da colei che fu nel mondo sola.

E per dir a l'estremo il gran servigio,
da mille atti inonesti l' ho ritratto,
ché mai per alcun patto
a lui piacer non poteo cosa vile:
giovene schivo e vergognoso in atto
126   et in penser, poi che fatto era uom ligio
di lei ch' alto vestigio
l' impresse al core e fecel suo simile;
quanto ha del pellegrino e del gentile,
da lei tene e da me di cui si biasma.
131   Mai notturno fantasma
d' error non fu sí pien, com' ei ver noi;
ch' è in grazia, da poi
che ne conobbe, a Dio et a la gente:
135   di ciò il superbo si lamenta e pente.

Ancor, e questo è quel che tutto avanza,
da volar sopra 'l ciel li avea dat' ali
per le cose mortali,
che son scala al Fattor, chi ben l' estima:
ché, mirando ei ben fiso quante e quali
141   eran vertuti in quella sua speranza,
d' una in altra sembianza
potea levarsi a l' alta cagion prima:
ed ei l' ha detto alcuna volta in rima.
Or m' ha posto in oblio con quella donna
146   ch' i' li die' per colonna
de la sua frale vita». A questo, un strido
lagrimoso alzo, e grido:
«Ben me la die', ma tosto la ritolse».
150   Responde: «Io no, ma chi per sé la volse».

Alfin ambo conversi al giusto seggio,
i' con tremanti, ei con voci alte e crude,
ciascun per sé conclude:
«Nobile donna, tua sentenzia attendo».
Ella allor sorridendo:
156   «Piacemi aver vostre questioni udite;
ma piú tempo bisogna a tanta lite».

58 (CCCLXIV)

Tennemi amor anni ventuno ardendo,
lieto nel foco e nel duol pien di speme;
poi che madonna e 'l mio cor seco inseme
4   saliro al ciel, dieci altri anni piangendo;

omai son stanco, e mia vita reprendo
di tanto error, che di vertute il seme
ha quasi spento, e le mie parti estreme,
8   alto Dio, a te devotamente rendo,

pentito e tristo de' miei sí spesi anni,
che spender si deveano in miglior uso,
11   in cercar pace ed in fuggir affanni.

Signor, che 'n questo carcer m' hai rinchiuso,
tramene salvo da li eterni danni,
14   ch' i' conosco 'l mio fallo e non lo scuso.

59 (CCCLXV)

I' vo piangendo i miei passati tempi,
i quai posi in amar cosa mortale,
senza levarmi a volo, abbiend' io l' ale
4   per dar forse di me non bassi esempi.

Tu che vedi i miei mali indegni et empi,
Re del cielo, invisibile, immortale,
soccorri a l' alma disviata e frale,
8   e 'l suo defetto di tua grazia adempi;

sí che, s' io vissi in guerra ed in tempesta,
mora in pace ed in porto, e se la stanza
11   fu vana, almen sia la partita onesta.

A quel poco di viver che m' avanza
ed al morir degni esser tua man presta:
14   tu sai ben che 'n altrui non ho speranza.

60 (CCCLXVI)

Vergine bella, che di sol vestita,
coronata di stelle, al sommo Sole
piacesti sí che 'n te sua luce ascose,
amor mi spinge a dir di te parole;
ma non so 'ncominciar senza tu' aita
6   e di colui ch' amando in te si pose.
Invoco lei che ben sempre rispose,
chi la chiamò con fede.
Vergine, s' a mercede
miseria estrema de l' umane cose
già mai ti volse, al mio prego t' inchina:
soccorri a la mia guerra,
13   ben chi' i' sia terra   e tu del ciel regina.

Vergine saggia e del bel numero una
de le beate vergini prudenti,
anzi la prima e con piú chiara lampa;
o saldo scudo de le afflitte genti
contr' a' colpi di morte e di fortuna,
19   sotto 'l qual si triunfa, non pur scampa;
o refrigerio al cieco ardor ch' avvampa
qui fra i mortali sciocchi;
Vergine, que' belli occhi
che vider tristi la spietata stampa
ne' dolci membri del tuo caro figlio,
volgi al mio dubio stato
26   che sconsigliato   a te ven per consiglio.

Vergine pura, d' ogni parte intera,
del tuo parto gentil figliuola e madre,
ch' allumi questa vita e l' altra adorni,
per te il tuo Figlio e quel del sommo Padre,
o fenestra del ciel lucente, altera,
32   venne a salvarne in su li estremi giorni;

e fra tutt' i terreni altri soggiorni
sola tu fosti eletta,
Vergine benedetta,
che 'l pianto d' Eva in allegrezza torni.
Fammi, ché puoi, de la sua grazia degno,
senza fine o beata,
39   già coronata   nel superno regno.

Vergine santa, d' ogni grazia piena,
che per vera ed altissima umiltate
salisti al ciel, onde miei preghi ascolti,
tu partoristi il fonte di pietate
e di giustizia il sol, che rasserena
45   il secol pien d' errori oscuri e folti:
tre dolci e cari nomi hai in te raccolti,
madre, figliuola e sposa,
Vergine gloriosa,
donna del Re che nostri lacci ha sciolti
e fatto 'l mondo libero e felice,
ne le cui sante piaghe
52   prego ch' appaghe   il cor, vera beatrice.

Vergine sola al mondo, senza esempio,
che 'l ciel di tue bellezze innamorasti,
cui né prima fu simil, né seconda,
santi penseri, atti pietosi e casti
al vero Dio sacrato e vivo tempio
58   fecero in tua verginità feconda.
Per te po la mia vita esser ioconda,
s' a' tuoi preghi, o Maria,
Vergine dolce e pia,
ove 'l fallo abondò la grazia abonda.
Con le ginocchia de la mente inchine,
prego che sia mia scorta
65   e la mia torta   via drizzi a buon fine.

Vergine chiara e stabile in eterno,
di questo tempestoso mare stella,

d'ogni fedel nocchier fidata guida,
pon mente in che terribile procella
i' mi ritrovo sol, senza governo,
71   ed ho già da vicin l' ultime strida.
Ma pur in te l' anima mia si fida,
peccatrice, i' nol nego,
Vergine, ma ti prego
che 'l tuo nemico del mio mal non rida.
Ricorditi che fece il peccar nostro
prender Dio, per scamparne,
78   umana carne   al tuo virginal chiostro.

Vergine, quante lagrime ho già sparte,
quante lusinghe e quanti preghi indarno,
pur per mia pena e per mio grave danno!
Da poi ch' i' nacqui in su la riva d'Arno,
cercando or questa ed or quell'altra parte,
84   non è stata mia vita altro ch' affanno;
mortal bellezza, atti e parole m' hanno
tutta ingombrata l' alma.
Vergine sacra ed alma,
non tardar, ch' i' son forse a l' ultimo anno:
i dí miei, piú correnti che saetta,
fra miserie e peccati
91   sonsen andati,   e sol morte n' aspetta.

Vergine, tale è terra e posto ha in doglia
lo mio cor, che vivendo in pianto il tenne,
e de mille miei mali un non sapea;
e, per saperlo, pur quel che n' avvenne
fora avvenuto, ch' ogni altra sua voglia
97   era a me morte ed a lei fama rea.
Or tu, Donna del ciel, tu, nostra Dea,
se dir lice e convensi,
Vergine d' alti sensi,
tu vedi il tutto, e quel che non potea
far altri è nulla a la tua gran vertute:

por fine al mio dolore,
104 ch' a te onore   ed a me fia salute.

Vergine, in cui ho tutta mia speranza,
che possi e vogli al gran bisogno aitarme,
non mi lasciare in su l' estremo passo;
non guardar me, ma chi degnò crearme;
no 'l mio valor, ma l' alta sua sembianza
110 ch' è in me ti mova a curar d' uom sí basso.
Medusa e l' error mio m' han fatto un sasso
d' umor vano stillante:
Vergine, tu di sante
lagrime e pie adempi 'l meo cor lasso,
ch' almen l' ultimo pianto sia devoto,
senza terrestro limo,
117 come fu 'l primo   non d' insania voto.

Vergine umana e nemica d' orgoglio,
del comune principio amor t' induca;
miserere d' un cor contrito, umile,
ché, se poca mortal terra caduca
amar con sí mirabil fede soglio,
123 che devrò far di te, cosa gentile?
Se dal mio stato assai misero e vile
per le tue man resurgo,
Vergine, i' sacro e purgo
al tuo nome e pensieri e 'ngegno e stile,
la lingua e 'l cor, le lagrime e i sospiri:
scorgimi al miglior guado
130 e prendi in grado   i cangiati desiri.

Il dí s' appressa e non pote esser lunge,
sí corre il tempo e vola,
Vergine unica e sola,
e 'l cor or conscienzia or morte punge:
raccomandami al tuo Figliuol, verace
omo e verace Dio,
137 ch' accolga 'l mio   spirto ultimo in pace.

ABBREVIATIONS

in notes and vocabulary

adj.	adjective
adv.	adverb
conj.	conjunction
def.	definite
dem.	demonstrative
dim.	diminutive
f.	feminine
fig.	figurative
imp.	imperative
indic.	indicative
m.	masculine
perf.	perfect
pers.	person
pl.	plural
p.p.	past participle
pres.	present
subj.	subjective

NOTES

I (I)

This sonnet serves as an introduction to the *Canzoniere*. In it Petrarch admits the folly of his youth, and asks his readers for their pity: with the coming of maturity he has realised the vanity of all worldly desires.

1   **rime sparse**: i.e. not forming a continuous whole, unlike the *Divine Comedy* or the *Aeneid*. The original manuscript and the earliest printed editions are entitled 'Francisci Petrarche laureati poete Rerum vulgarium fragmenta'.

3   **in sul**: 'during'.

giovenile errore: for the exact date on which Petrarch fell in love see no. 2 in this anthology (III).

4   **era**: 'I was'. The reader should note that here and in other verbs he will find -*a* in the *first* pers. of the imperfect indic.

7   **ove**: 'wherever'.

9–10   cf. Horace, *Epodes*, XI, 7–8:

> Heu me, per urbem, nam pudet tanti mali,
> Fabula quanta fui!

'Alas, for I am ashamed of so great a wrong, how great a scandal I was throughout the city.'

14   This last line gives splendid expression to a judgement that sums up the experiences expressed in the *Rime*; it is a theme that recurs frequently in them.

NOTES

2 (III)

Petrarch tells how he fell in love with Laura on the anniversary of the Crucifixion of Christ.

1-2 'It was the day on which the rays of the sun lost their brightness because of the suffering of his Maker', i.e. the anniversary of Christ's death. According to the Gospels, there was darkness when He was crucified: 'Now from the sixth hour there was darkness over all the land unto the ninth hour' (*Matthew*, XXVII, 45). In the note he made in his Virgil (which we have quoted in our introduction), Petrarch wrote that he fell in love on April 6th, 1327. This he repeated in poem CCXI, 12-14:

> Mille trecento ventisette, a punto
> su l'ora prima il dí sesto d'aprile
> nel laberinto entrai, né veggio ond'esca.

C. Calcaterra (in *La data fatale nel Canzoniere e nei Trionfi del Petrarca*, Turin, 1926) explained that Petrarch was thinking of the actual date on which Christ died (*feria sexta aprilis*, according to tradition), not of the movable date of Good Friday, which, as has often been pointed out, fell on 10th April in 1327.

scoloraro: 3rd pers. plural past def. like *legaro* (l. 4) and *s'incominciaro* (l. 8).

5 **parea:** *pareva* in modern Italian.

6 **però:** 'for that reason'.

7-8 **onde i miei guai . . .:** 'therefore my woes had their beginning in our common grief', i.e. on the day when all Christians grieved on account of Christ's suffering.

9 **Trovommi:** *mi trovò*.

12–14 'So, in my view, it was not to his [i.e. love's] credit that he should have wounded me with his arrow while I was in that state (i.e. *disarmato*, l. 9), while you, who were armed, were not even shown his bow.' **li** = *gli*.

3 (XII)

When age has destroyed Laura's beauty, the poet will at last have courage enough to express his sufferings, and she will have pity on him. But, it is implied, it will be too late.

2 **schermire:** 'to defend from': to be taken with *da l'aspro tormento* and *dagli affanni.*

3 **per vertú degli:** 'because of the': the phrase is dependent on *spento* in l. 4.

4 **lume spento:** this means that Laura's eyes will lose their sparkle, not that she will go blind.

5 **cape':** modern: *capelli.*

6 **voi** is to be understood.

9 **pur:** 'yet, finally'.

10 **de' miei martiri:** dependent on *gli anni e i giorni e l'ore.*

12 **tempo:** old age.

4 (XVI)

Just as the old pilgrim, overcoming all obstacles, goes to Rome to see the image of Christ in the Veronica, so the poet seeks in others the image of his lady.

1 **bianco:** most probably a reiteration of the idea contained in 'canuto', although one could also take *canuto* to refer to the colour of his hair, *bianco* to that of his face.

2 **ov' ha sua età fornita:** *fornire* in Old Italian often means 'to complete'. According to De Sanctis (*Saggio*, p. 99), 'frase dubbia e molto poetica, che ti presenta insieme due idee, cioè che ha passato colà tutta la sua vita, e che questa vita si può dir già finita, non restandogli che poco altro a vivere.'

4 **venir manco:** 'to fail it, leave': *manco = meno.*

10 **la sembianza di Colui:** the Veronica: the veil or cloth which is supposed to preserve the image of the face of Christ. According to tradition, St. Veronica was a woman of Jerusalem who took pity on Christ as he struggled with His heavy cross and wiped His sweating face with a cloth. On this cloth there was miraculously imprinted an image of His features. A cloth, supposed to be 'Veronica's veil' is preserved in St. Peter's, Rome. Cf. Dante, *Par.*, XXXI, 104.

5 (XXII)

All the beasts of the earth rest during the night, but the poet suffers both night and day because of Laura's cruelty, and knows only too well that whatever hopes he may have of her relenting will never be realised.

2 **se non se:** 'except'.

5 **qual torna a casa:** i.e. men and their domestic animals.
qual . . . qual: 'one . . . another'.

8 **scuoter:** 'disperse'.

14 i.e. when it is dawn at the other side of the world, in the Antipodes.

17 **ch' i' vidi 'l sole:** In view of the fact that Laura is certainly the *si aspra fera* of l. 20, it seems best, in order not to make Petrarch guilty of the jarring juxtaposition of two allegorical images, to understand by this phrase 'that I saw the sun' i.e. 'was born', not 'that I saw Laura'.

18 **che** refers to the content of stanzas 2 and 3 as a whole.

22 **non mi stanca:** i.e. of weeping. **primo sonno:** i.e. the beginning of the night.
Early night and dawn were according to ancient ideas the periods of deepest sleep. Cf. *Aen.*, I, 470: *primo quae prodita somno*: 'which betrayed in their first sleep'.

25 A reference to the Platonic doctrine that the soul comes from a particular star and after death returns there. Cf. *Par.*, IV, 52.

26 **tomi:** 'fall'.
l'amorosa selva: In Virgil's underworld those who loved unhappily in this life wander, still suffering, in a myrtle wood.

> Hic quos durus amor crudeli tabe peredit
> secreti celant calles et myrtea circum
> silva tegit.   (*Aen.*, VI, 442–4):

'Here those whom harsh love consumed with its cruel wasting are concealed by secret paths and surrounded by a myrtle wood.'

Presumably Petrarch has Virgil's wood in mind rather than the pains of Hell.

27 **trita terra:** i.e. dust.

33 **e mai non fosse l'alba:** i.e. that the night should be endless.

34 **se:** refl. pron.

34 **in verde selva:** i.e. *in lauro*. Here as elsewhere Petrarch identifies Laura with the laurel tree, and refers to the myth of Daphne. Daphne (δάφνη—'laurel') resisted the advances of Apollo, and ran away from him: when Apollo caught up with her on the banks of the River Peneus, she prayed to Zeus for rescue: she immediately became a laurel tree. (Ovid, *Met.*, 1, 550.)

37 **in secca selva:** 'in dry wood', i.e. in a coffin.

6 (XXIII)

In this, frequently called the canzone of the metamorphoses, the poet tells the story of his love for Laura. When he has described his condition in the days when he scorned love, he symbolises his falling in love with Laura by transformation of himself into a laurel. There follow his metamorphoses into a swan, a stone, a fountain, an echo and a stag.

1-6 Begin construing in l. 4: 'Since, by singing of it, one obtains relief from one's pain, I shall sing of how I lived in freedom while love was disdained by me [here return to l. 1:] in the sweet years of my youth (*prima etade*), which saw . . .', etc.

8 **altamente:** 'profoundly'.

14 **ch' acquistan fede a la penosa vita:** 'which demonstrate how wretched my life is.'

16 **iscusilla** = *iscusinla* = *la scusino*. The subject is *i martiri et un penser*. The meaning of ll. 15–18 is: 'And if memory here does not come to my aid, as it usually does, let it be excused because of my torments and because of a thought which alone gives it such pain that . . .'

17 **dàlle** = *le dà*.

21-2 'I say that many years had passed since the day when love first assailed me', i.e. since his adolescence, when he first discovered the nature of love.

26 **il duro affetto:** the determination not to fall in love

31 **La vita el fin, e 'l dí loda la sera:** 'the end praise life and the evening praises day', i.e. only at the end of a life is one in a position to judge it, an adaptation of Ovid's *Exitu acta probat*, 'the value of actions is determined by their result. (*Her.*, II, 85.)

38 **ei duo:** love and Laura (the *possente donna* of l. 35).

48 **Peneo:** see note to 5 (XXII), 34.
piú altero fiume: the Rhone or the Durance.

50-60 The poet had hoped to enjoy Laura's love; his hope had been excessive. He therefore compares his hope to Phaethon, son of Helios (the Sun). In spite of Helios's warning, Phaethon tried to drive his father's chariot, but he proved incapable of guiding the horses of the Sun. When they bolted and there was a risk of the earth being burnt, Zeus hurled a thunderbolt at Phaethon, who fell into the river Eridanus, normally taken to be the Po. When Cycnus sought and wept for his friend and relation, Phaethon, Cycnus was metamorphosed into a swan. (See Ovid, *Met.*, II, 371.) Here the poet is changed into a swan after the death of his hope.

60 **col suon:** 'as the singing progressed', i.e. when he became a poet.

67 'What must it have been like to experience it, if the mere memory of it torments me?'

69 **dolce et acerba mia nemica:** Laura. The 'sweet enemy' (previously the *douza ennemia* of the Provençal poets) was to become a frequent ingredient of Petrarchist verse.

71 'although it is such as to exceed all expression of it.'

72 **Questa:** the 'sweet enemy' of l. 69.

72–4 Of the various interpretations offered of these lines, the likeliest seems to be that Laura forbade Petrarch to speak of his love for her.

75–80 After forbidding the poet to speak of his love, Laura appeared to him in another guise, when, not knowing her, he revealed the truth to her. Assuming her previous aspect, she turned him into a stone (albeit a living and frightened one). The myth here paralleled is that of the shepherd Battus. When Mercury stole Apollo's cows, Battus promised not to reveal what he knew. Mercury appeared to the shepherd in another form, and offered him a reward for the information. When Battus broke his promise by giving it, Mercury turned him into a stone. (See Ovid, *Met.*, II, 685.)

82 **fea:** *faceva.*

84 **spetra:** lit. 'unstones', i.e. 'releases me from my petrified state'.

86 'Return, my lord (=love), to make me weep', i.e. let me go back to my previous, miserable state rather than remain in this stony condition.

102   **così:** by means of his humble verse.

112–17   Here the poet imitates the metamorphosis of Biblis. She, searching for her lover, who was fleeing from her, wept copiously, and was turned into a fountain. (See Ovid, *Met.*, IX, 640.)

118   **tenni quel viaggio:** 'I flowed in that way'.

128   **in lui:** i.e. in its Maker, God.

129   'and she does so, in order that sin should be more feared'. **pavente:** pres. subj. form common in Italian at this period. See also *fide* (l. 136).

fal = '*lo fa*'.

137   **ripregando:** 'when I renewed my pleading'.

137–40   Here there is a reminiscence of the metamorphosis of Echo. Rejected by Narcissus, she pined away until nothing remained of her but her voice. (Ovid, *Met.*, II, 390.)

138   **scossa:** 'deprived of, cut off from' (Latin *excussus*).

139   **antiche some:** 'former body'.

140   **lei:** Laura.

154–60   The poet, after telling how he came upon Laura naked in a spring, imitates the metamorphosis of Actaeon, who, having similarly disconcerted Diana when she was bathing, was turned into a stag and torn apart by his own hounds. (See Ovid, *Met.*, III, 183.) Petrarch's dogs (l. 160) are probably his thoughts.

157   '. . . that I seemed to leave my own body'.

161   This is a reference to the myth of Danae, who was shut up in a tower in order that none should visit her. But Jupiter loved her and came to her in a shower of gold. Their son was Perseus.

163   '**l foco di Giove**: Jupiter changed into fire for love of Aegina. For both transformations (gold and fire), see Ovid. (*Met.*, VI, 113.)

165   **l'uccel**: the eagle. Jupiter became one in order to carry off Asteria.

169   **piacer**: probably 'beauty'. Cf. *Inf.*, V, 104.

7 (XXXV)

He shuns the company of men, ashamed that they may see how he suffers for love. But however wild and deserted the places he chooses, love never leaves him.

3-4   'And I watch attentively for where any human footstep may print the ground (*arena*), so as to escape (*per fuggire*)'.

7   **negli atti d'allegrezza spenti**: 'in my actions devoid of joy'.

11   **altrui**: 'from men'.

14   **con meco**: i.e. *con me*. The *-co* of *meco* is pleonastic.

8 (L)

In the evening the tired old woman on a pilgrimage, the labourer returning from the fields to his frugal supper, the shepherd spreading rushes on the floor of his hut or cave, the sailors putting into a quiet inlet for the night, all find peace. But not the poet; as darkness falls, his torment increases.

1 **stagion:** here 'the time of day': **che 'l ciel rapido inchina / verso occidente,** 'when the sun is fast going down in the West'.

13–14 '. . . increases whenever the eternal light [i.e. the sun] prepares to leave us.'

16–17 **...onde discende / dagli altissimi monti maggior l'ombra:** 'because of which the shadow falls longer from the very high mountains', almost a translation of Virgil's *maioresque cadunt altis de montibus umbrae* (*Eclogues*, 1, 83).

18 **avaro zappador:** the adjective follows Virgil's *avari agricolae* (*Georg.*, 1, 47.)

23 '. . . like those acorns (hence, frugality) to which all pay tribute, but which all avoid', a reference to Man's ability to subsist on acorns in the Golden Age. Cf. 24 (CXXXVI), 2.

28 i.e. neither because of a change of day nor because of a change of season.

39 **informe,** 2nd pers. sing., hence here: 'you induce me, drive me to . . .'

43–5 **in qualche chiusa valle:** 'in some sheltered fjord'. These lines closely follow Virgil's

> . . . placida laxabant membra quiete
> sub remis fusi per dura sedilia nautae (*Aen*, v. 836–7).

'Sprawled on their hard benches under their oars, the sailors relaxed their limbs in peaceful rest.'

46 **perché s'attuffi:** 'although it [the sun] goes down . . .'.

48 **le Colonne:** the pillars of Hercules, the Straits of Gibraltar.

61   **quando che sia:** 'at any time.'

63–70...**che volli...**: 'what did I bring upon myself [lit. 'wish for, will'] when I first gazed so fixedly [lit. 'held them', i.e. the 'eyes' referred to in l. 62] on that fair face, in order that it should be impressed by the imagination on that place [i.e. in his heart] from which neither force nor art will be able to move it until I become the prey of her who takes all away? Nor do I know what I should think of her [fem. pron. standing for *la morte*, i.e. whether I should believe that even death will be able to obliterate it].'

77   i.e. 'to what a condition I have been reduced by the fire . . .'

78   **viva petra:** Laura is hard as a stone.

9 (LII)

The poet is overwhelmed when he sees his beloved washing a veil.

1   **al suo amante:** i.e. Actaeon. See note to no. 6, ll. 154–60.

2   **per tal ventura:** i.e. through a stroke of fortune similar to his own.

4   **ch' a me:** dependent on *più* (l. 1) 'than did please me . . .'
la pastorella: i.e. Laura. She becomes a shepherdess here because the madrigal was in origin a popular form and, therefore, popular, if idyllic, images were associated with it.

6   **a l'aura:** a pun on the name Laura.

7   **egli arde 'l cielo:** the *egli* is pleonastic; 'when the sky burns'.

IO (LIII)

This canzone is addressed to a statesman to whom Petrarch looks for the leadership necessary to the resurgence of Rome and of Italy. Who this man was is not known. Various candidates have been proposed for the honour, among them Cola di Rienzo, Stefano Colonna the Elder, Stefano Colonna the Younger and Paolo Annibaldi. The most likely of the names suggested is perhaps that of Bosone da Gubbio, elected Roman senator on 15th October, 1337.

1-3 'Noble spirit, directing those limbs within which on his pilgrimage [through life] lives a gentleman who is . . .'

4 **onorata verga:** the sceptre of a Roman senator.

5 **erranti:** the citizens of Rome who go astray.

10 'I know not what Italy expects or longs for . . .'

14 'Would that I had my hands wrapped in her hair', i.e. that I might pull her up and shake her.

18 'It is not without destiny', i.e. it is clearly destined that . . .

20 **il nostro capo Roma:** cf. Livy, 1, 16: *ut mea Roma caput orbis terrarum sit:* 'in order that my Rome be capital of the world'.

26-8 **'l popol di Marte:** the Romans. 'For if the Roman people should look again to its own honour, it seems to me that this grace may be granted in your days' (i.e. under your leadership).

29-30 'The ancient walls, which the world fears and loves,

and trembles at still . . .'; *trema* is used transitively like the
teme and *ama* it follows.

32   **i sassi:** here, the graves.

33   **di ta':** of the great Romans of antiquity.

36   **saldar ogni suo vizio:** 'set it all to rights', lit. 'make
good every crack in it' (Lat. *vitium*).

37   **O grandi Scipioni:** Scipio Africanus Maior and Scipio
Africanus Minor. The former, by his victory at Zama in
202 B.C. brought the Second Punic War to an end. The latter
finally destroyed Carthage in 146 B.C.

o fedel Bruto: Lucius Junius Brutus, whose fidelity was such
that he is said to have put his own sons to death when they
conspired to restore the Tarquins.

39   **ben locato offizio:** probably the office of Roman
senator.

40   **cre'** = *credo*.

Fabrizio: Gaius Fabricius Luscinus, a man celebrated for
incorruptibility. Sent to Pyrrhus as ambassador in the winter
of 280–279 B.C., he resisted all the attempts to corrupt him.
And in 278 he sent back to Pyrrhus the traitor who had offered
to poison him.

43   cf. Virgil, *Aen.*, II, 536: *si qua est coelo pietas quae
talia curet:* 'if there is any justice in heaven, which attends to
such things'.

48   **tetti:** here the poet is referring to the churches.

50   **spelunca di ladron:** cf. *Luke*, XIX, 46, 'My house is
the house of prayer: but ye have made of it a den of thieves'.

55-6 **Né senza squille:** the meaning is that even the church bells, placed where they are for purposes of thanksgiving, are used as signals for assault by the bands of miscreants who meet in God's house to plan their crimes.

57-8 cf. Virgil, *Aen.*, XII, 131-2:

> tum studio effusae matres et volgus inermum
> invalidique senes . . .

'then mothers eagerly rushing out and the defenceless crowd and feeble old men.'

71 **Orsi, lupi, leoni, aquile e serpi:** the poet here alludes, by reference to their coats of arms, to the families who opposed the Colonna: *Orsi:* the Orsini; *lupi, aquile:* two branches of the family of the Counts of Tusculum; *leoni:* the Savelli; *serpi:* the Caetani.

74 **quella gentil donna:** Rome.

77 **piú che 'l millesimo anno:** in A.D. 330 Constantine transferred the seat of government of the Empire to Byzantium, which was renamed Constantinople.

82 **Tu marito, tu padre:** the statesman addressed in this poem is to be the husband of Rome, the father of Italy. For, now that the papal court is in Avignon, Rome has neither pope nor emperor.

84 **ché 'l maggior padre:** Pope Benedict XII, whom Petrarch would have liked to see restoring the papacy to Rome, was intent instead on building a sumptuous palace at Avignon (1334-7). To him Petrarch had addressed in vain a verse epistle depicting Rome in her widowed state.

88-9 'Now, by clearing the way by which you came to

power, she (Fortune) obtains a pardon from me for her other offences.'

fammisi perdonar: *si fa perdonare da me.*

94-5   **drizzar…in stato:** restore to dignity.

97   **aitar:** *aiutarono.*

99   **Sopra 'l monte Tarpeio:** on the Capitol. The reference is to the Tarpeian rock at the south-west corner of the Capitoline hill.

I I (LXI)

A benediction of his love and all that has come from it whether painful or pleasant.

2   **e 'l tempo:** i.e. the part of the day.

3   **giunto:** 'caught'.

6   **ch' i' ebbi** etc.: 'when I was compelled to be joined with love'.

13   **l'acquisto:** *le acquisto.*

I2 (LXII)

It is the eleventh anniversary of the day on which Petrarch saw Laura. He prays God to release him from his passion in order that he may turn to worthier concerns.

1   **perduti giorni:** i.e. days which could have been put to better use.

4   The poet has spent his time contemplating the person and ways of Laura which, unfortunately for him (*per mio mal*), are very beautiful.

5   **col tuo lume:** 'with Your light', i.e. by means of God's grace.

8   **adversario:** the Devil.

9   **l'undecimo anno:** eleven years have passed since the day on which he saw Laura. (See the reference to the day in l. 14. See also notes to sonnet III of the *Canzoniere*, no. 2 in this anthology.)

12   **non degno:** it is not worthy of a Christian to have been so concerned with wordly passion.

13-14   He beseeches God, in order to lead his (Petrarch's) thoughts back to worthier subjects, to remind them that today He was crucified.

13 (LXX)

Although the poet's prayers go unanswered, he will still ask love for eventual happiness, even if such happiness could never balance his sufferings. But he knows that he is dreaming: Laura is completely indifferent to him. For her indifference he should blame not his destiny but himself, for being incapable of appreciating her true beauty, and deriving benefit from it.

3   **ascolte:** pres. subjunctive.

5   **egli:** impersonal.

5-7   'But if I am to be permitted to end these laments (*voci meschine*) before my death (*fine*) . . .

8 **non gravi:** i.e. *non sia grave.*

signor: i.e. love.

10 'It is right and just that I should sing and take my
pleasure.' The first line of a well-known canzone concludes
each stanza: this line is most probably from a poem by Arnaut
Daniel; see the Introduction. Cf. *Trionfo d'Amore*, III, 40 and
Purg., XXVI, 115. Petrarch was not the first poet to combine
two languages in one poem: Dante had written a canzone in
three languages, and the troubadour Raimbaut de Vaqueiras
one in four.

12 **però c'ho:** 'because I have': *c'* is *che.*

15 **potesse:** modern *potessi.*

17 **detto:** 'verse': so in l. 20 **dire** 'to speak in verse'.

20 'My lady begs me (i.e. to speak): for which reason I
wish to speak.' The first line of the famous canzone by Guido
Cavalcanti, for whom see the Introduction.

24 **per me:** 'by my own efforts'.

nol: *non lo*

28 **pur:** 'always'.

30 The opening line of Dante, *Rime*, CIII.

31 Based upon the words of Dido in Virgil, *Aen.*, IV, 595:

Quid loquor? aut ubi sum? Quae mentem insania mutat?
'What am I saying? Where am I? What madness affects my
mind?'

33 **trascorro:** i.e. with the eyes.

34   Contrast this with 5 (XXII), 24, where he holds the stars responsible for his fate.

37   **de le cose belle:** this presumably refers to Laura rather than the stars.

39   **grave:** 'laden'.

40   The opening line of a canzone by Cino da Pistoia; see Introduction.

39–40   Construe: *La dolce vista e 'l bel guardo soave mi fe' gir grave del suo piacer.*
piacer: 'beauty'.

42   cf. *Genesis* I, 31. 'And God saw everything that he had made, and behold, it was very good.'

43–44   i.e. he is incapable of perceiving inner beauty since he is dazzled by the outer.

45   **vero splendor:** i.e. spiritual splendour.

46   **fermo:** i.e. too weak to bear the sight of her spiritual beauty.

50   The first line of one of Petrarch's own canzoni (*Rime*, XXIII, no. 6 in this anthology).

14 (LXXII)

The second of three canzoni (LXXI, LXXII, LXXIII) which Petrarch wrote in praise of his lady's eyes, this poem concentrates on the beneficent effects of his love for Laura: the

light from her eyes raises his mind to heavenly things, the
sight of them inspires him to win glory by his work on earth.

4–6   literally: 'And through long-established custom, there
within, where I sit alone with love, almost visibly the heart
shines through', i.e. because of the poet's familiarity with them,
he can almost see in Laura's eyes the workings of her heart.

8   **glorioso fine:** Two interpretations are possible: that the
glorioso fine is beatitude (an interpretation in keeping with the
statement already made that the light from Laura's eyes shows
Petrarch the way to heaven) or that it refers to earthly glory.
The latter seems more probable. Petrarch in the first stanza
wishes to mention the good effects of Laura's inspiration in
relation both to eternal life (which he has already done) and
to life on earth (which he is now doing); he will then develop
each of these points in turn later in the poem.

10–11   'Nor could human tongue ever tell . . .'

14–15   i.e. in spring, the season of his first sight of Laura.

17   **motor eterno:** God.

18   'deigned to display some of his work on earth'.

22   **la mia usata guerra:** i.e. his passion for Laura.

26   **'nsin allor:** i.e. before he fell in love with Laura.

31–5   'Nor did love or fickle fortune ever grant a state so
joyous to their favourites in the world that I should not be
willing to exchange it for a glance from those eyes whence . . .'

45   **rimanse:** *si rimane.* The *si* is pleonastic.

50   **tra 'l bel nero e 'l bianco:** 'between the beautiful
black (of the pupils) and the white'.

52   **...da le fasce e da la culla:** 'from the time when I

was in my swaddling-clothes and my cradle': the poet is saying
that he believes that Heaven had from his infancy prepared to
provide this remedy (the sight of Laura's eyes) for the poet's
imperfection and the adversity of fortune.

55–8 Petrarch complains that he is wronged by Laura's
veil and by her hand, so often interposed between his greatest
delight (Laura's eyes) and *his* eyes.

58 **onde:** 'from which [the poet's eyes] pours out . . .'

60 The poet's heart varies in relation to Laura's aspect,
i.e. according to whether her attitude to the poet seems kind
or harsh.

62 'that my natural endowment is not enough, and does not
make me worthy of . . .'

66 **foco gentil:** i.e. noble love. The word *gentil* here is but
one of the features in this poem which recall the poets of the
dolce stil novo, for the whole composition stresses the beneficial
effects of love, which brings out the lover's virtues.

67–71 Petrarch expresses the hope that if, through eager
endeavour, he can make himself swift to embrace good, and
slow to do the opposite, despising everything that the world
desires, the fame of being such a person may help him to win
favourable judgement from Laura.

72–5 'Certainly the end to my tears, which my grief-
stricken heart calls for from no other place, comes from those
beautiful eyes at last gently twinkling, the final hope of
courteous lovers'.

76 **l'una sorella:** the first of the three canzoni on Laura's
eyes.

77 **e l'altra:** the last of the three.

78 **ond' io piú carta vergo:** 'so I go on writing'.

I 5 (LXXXI)

The first suggestion for this sonnet came perhaps from
Psalm LV, which Petrarch echoes in the last two lines; but,
whereas the Psalmist wished for the wings of a dove in order
that he might flee from his enemies and be at rest in the
wilderness, the poet, weary under the burden of his sins,
yearns to escape from the Devil's clutches and follow Christ.

1-2 **fascio:** the burden of the poet's sin and his deeply
rooted love for Laura. There are probably reminiscences of
Psalm XXXVIII here: 'For mine iniquities are gone over mine
head: as an heavy burden they are too heavy for me . . . I am
troubled; I am bowed down greatly . . .'

4 **del mio nemico:** i.e. of the Devil.

5 The 'great friend' who came to deliver him was Christ.
This seems clear if we consider the words uttered by this friend
in lines 10–11. Nevertheless, some commentators have identi-
fied the *grande amico* with Petrarch's virtue or with prevenient
grace, while De Sade thought he was Father Dionigi da Borgo
S. Sepolcro, who invited the poet to Naples.

10–11 A paraphrase of *Matthew*, XI, 28: 'Come unto me,
all ye that labour and are heavy laden . . .'
se 'l passo altri non serra: 'if nobody bars the way,' a
phrase which echoes Dante's *venite a noi parlar, s'altri nol
niega* (*Inf.*, v, 81).

13–14 cf. 'And I said, Oh that I had wings like a dove, for
then would I fly away, and be at rest' (*Ps.*, LV, 6).

16 (XC)

The poet recalls the divine beauty of Laura, which first caused
him to fall in love with her, and remarks that, although that
beauty may have faded, his love has remained constant.

1   **a l'aura:** Petrarch again plays on the name Laura, as in
9 (LII), 6. For the image cf. *Aen.*, I, 319: *dederatque comas
diffundere ventis:* 'she had let the winds distress her hair'.
Petrarch's description of Laura in this sonnet and Virgil's
description of Venus as she appears to Aeneas (*Aen.*, I, 319–28)
have several elements in common.

2   **gli:** modern *li*.

3–4   cf. 3 (XII), 3–4.

5–6   'And, whether rightly or wrongly, I thought that pity
coloured her face' (literally, 'her face seemed to me to become
of piteous colours').

7   **esca:** 'tinder', i.e. he was by nature receptive to the
power of love.

11   **pur:** 'merely'. For the idea cf. *Aen.*, I, 328: *Nec vox
hominem sonat:* 'nor does the voice have a human sound'.

13   **e se non fosse or tale . . . :** 'and though now she may
not be so, my wound does not heal because of the slackening
of the bow'.

17 (CXXII)

Petrarch's passion for Laura has now lasted for seventeen years.
He wonders whether he will ever be free of it or whether his
love will ever become purely spiritual.

5–6   It is said of the wolf that he changes his coat, but not
his habits (*vezzo*): *il lupo cambia il pelo ma non il vizio.*

altri is here the equivalent of the French *on*.

6–7   **e, per lentar i sensi:** although the senses become
feebler with the years, human feelings do not become less
intense.

8   'That is done to us by the maleficent shadow of the
heavy veil' (i.e. the body, man's physical nature).

ne = *ci* 'us'.

9–11   'Alas, when will the day come when I, seeing the
years pass, emerge from . . .?'

12–14   The poet asks whether he will ever see the day when
Laura's beauty will please his eyes to the extent that he would
like (*quant' io vorrei*) and to the degree that is right (*quanto si
convene*), i.e. when her attraction for him will become entirely
spiritual.

18 (CXXIII)

As he is about to leave, Petrarch realises to his joy that Laura
regrets his departure.

1–2   **che 'l dolce riso,** etc.: 'which covered her smiling
face (*il dolce riso*, cf. *Inf.*, v, 133) with a mist of love'.

3   **al cor:** i.e. to the heart of Petrarch

s' offerse: subject: *quel vago impallidir* (l. 1).

4   literally: 'that my heart came to meet it through my face', i.e. 'that in response my emotions revealed themselves in my expression'.

5-6   A reference to the belief that the blessed in paradise communicate without words by means of the intellect alone.

8   'But I saw it, who do not gaze on any other thing'.

9   **vista:** 'expression'.

9-12   The expressions *angelica vista*, *atto umile*, *guardo gentile* are obvious echoes of the *dolce stil novo*: see Introduction.

19 (CXXV)

If Petrarch's verse were equal to his feelings, Laura would perhaps share his love. But his passion has deprived him of his poetic virtue; he can no longer give vent to his emotions in such attractive compositions as were inspired by love in his youth. Yet his imagination continues to present Laura's beauty to his mind. If she will not hear him, he will find consolation in nature, in the lovely places where he once saw her. There he loses himself in the pleasures of memory.

3   i.e. if his passion found suitable expression.

4   **tal:** Laura.

6   **desteriasi:** *si desterebbe*. 'And love would be awakened there (i.e. in Laura's heart) where it is now asleep'.

11   '. . . if she were to burn, who now seems of ice'.

14 **Però ch' amor:** 'Because love . . .'

20-2 **Miri:** singular verb with double subject: 'Let love and those lovely eyes in whose shadow he dwells look at what my heart holds'.

25-6 In the previous line Petrarch has mentioned his weeping (*pianto*) and the complaint he makes in his verse (*lamentar*). He now states that one of these (the weeping) hurts him, while the other (the lover's plaint) annoys another (i.e. Laura) because he is unable to express it subtly enough.

30 **squadre:** 3rd pers. sing. pres. subjunctive: 'who will break open . . .?'

33-5 'For I seem to have within it [i.e. in his heart, mentioned in l. 31] someone who is constantly painting my lady and speaking of her'.

38-9 The **soccorso** which he has lost is the ability to give vent to his feelings in the *dolci rime leggiadre* (l. 27) which he was able to write when love first assailed him.

49 'then [if Laura will not] do you listen, green bank . . .'
riva: the bank of the Sorgue.

58 **partir:** 'to share'.

59-60 'O that you had preserved some of the lovely scattered traces . . .'

64 **come po s' appaga:** 'consoles itself as best it can'. How it does so will be the subject of the next stanza.

68 **il vago lume:** i.e. of Laura's eyes.

77-8 'Blessed spirit of what kind are you when you have

this effect on others,' i.e. how wonderful Laura must be if thinking of her can give him such happiness.

79–81   The poet addresses the canzone he has just written, modestly pretending that it is a rough composition.

80   **credo che tel conoschi:** 'and I think you are aware of that'.

20 (CXXVI)

He addresses the various elements of an idyllic spot in which once he saw her, and reflects that, if he should die for love, he would prefer to be buried there. Perhaps Laura would return there, and, not finding him, sigh, and through that sigh win him grace in heaven. He returns in conclusion to his memories of Laura as she was on that day, and of his own exaltation.

2–3   There is no reason to suppose that Laura was not actually bathing, cf. 6 (XXIII), 150–1.
donna: here in the sense of *domina* i.e. a superior to whom subservience is due.

6   **fare...colonna:** i.e. to lean.

9   **seno:** either 'folds' (Latin *sinus*) or 'breast'.

14   **egli:** impersonal, cf. 9 (LII), 7.

16   **lagrimando:** modern *lacrimanti*.

17–18   'Let some grace [of heaven] bury my wretched body among you'.

19   **al proprio albergo:** see note to 5 (XXII), 25.
ignuda: i.e. free of the body.

22   **passo:** i.e. the transition from life to death.

29   cf. CXXXV, 45 where Laura becomes *questa fera angelica, innocente.*

30   **'v'** = *ove.*

34–5   **già terra infra le pietre / vedendo:** 'seeing that I am already earth among the stones [of the grave]' . . .

37   **impetre:** 3rd pers. sing. pres. subj.

38   **faccia forza al cielo:** 'do violence to heaven', i.e. to win pardon for him for his sins. Cf. *Matthew* XI, 12 'And from the days of John the Baptist until now the kingdom of heaven suffereth violence and the violent take it by force.'

48   **oro forbito e perle:** the *perle* refer either to the flowers in her hair or to the points in her hair which catch the light and therefore seem of a lighter colour.

56–61   'Her divine bearing, face, words and sweet laughter had so weighted me with forgetfulness (*carco d'oblio*) and so divided me from a true appraisal of what I saw (*da l'imagine vera*) that I said sighing . . .'

66   He addresses the poem: 'If you had as many refinements as you would like to have . . .'

68   cf. the conclusion of the preceding canzone. The two poems are clearly to be linked together.

2 I (CXXVIII)

Petrarch reproaches the rulers of Italy for their internecine strife and for their employment of foreign mercenaries. He urges them to rid their country's soil of the barbarian and to strive for peace. The composition of the poem probably belongs to 1344–5, when Petrarch found himself in besieged Parma (an experience he himself described in *Fam.*, v, 10).

1 **benché 'l parlar sia indarno:** 'although words are no remedy for . . .'

4–6 The poet is probably merely expressing the hope that his sighs will be such as Italy (here represented by three of her major rivers) expects of him. He refers to himself as being seated on the banks of the Po because he is in Lombardy.

12–14 '. . . and the hearts which proud, cruel Mars hardens and closes, do you, o Father, make tender and open',

15 **ivi:** i.e. in the hardened hearts.

16 **qual io mi sia:** 'however unworthy I may be . . .'

17 **Voi:** the rulers of Italy.

20 **tante pellegrine spade:** the swords are referred to as *pellegrine* because they are those of foreign soldiers.

25 **'n cor venale:** the hearts are venal because they are those of mercenaries.

26–7 Whoever has the greatest number of soldiers (i.e. of foreign mercenaries) is most surrounded by enemies.

31–2 'If this happens to us as the result of our own efforts, who is to save us?'

33–8 Nature had made provision for the well-being of Italy by placing the shield of the Alps between her and German fury, but the blind greed of Italian princelings who wanted to

indulge in fratricidal wars for the sake of personal aggrandise-
ment, had sacrificed the benefits of Nature's wisdom by
importing barbarian soldiers from the north.

40   The *fiere selvagge* are foreign soldiers and the *mansuete
gregge* the native population.

42–8   Petrarch argues that it is all the more painful that
Italians should have to suffer at the hands of descendants of
those lawless hordes whom Marius had so severely dealt with.
The reference is to Marius's defeat of the Teutones and
Cimbri at Aquae Sextiae (Aix-en-Provence) and Vercellae
(Vercelli) in 102 and 101 B.C. Florus, III, 3 (quoted by Petrarch,
Fam., XXII, 14) had asserted that at Aix the thirsty Roman
victor had drunk, not water, but blood from the river.

49–51   And the poet will say nothing of Caesar, who in
every country (*piaggia*) to which he led Roman soldiers (*ferro*
'iron' = 'the sword' and here stands for arms generally) made
the grass red with their blood.

53   **n' aggia:** *ci abbia*.

57–59   'What sin [of men's], what judgement [of God's],
what destiny [cause you] to oppress your poor neighbour . . .'
etc.

66   **bavarico:** because there were many Bavarian
mercenaries.

67   **ch' alzando il dito...:** The mercenaries raised their
fingers as a sign of surrender. They were also apt to make a
pretence of fighting (hence *colla morte scherza*) and to pass
from one side to the other.

68   **strazio:** here 'shame'.

69-70 'But your blood flows more freely; for another anger drives you', i.e. because you are taking seriously the fighting of which they are making a game.

71   **terza:** terce, the third hour of the canonical day, a good time for sober consideration.

72-3 **e vederete come...:** 'and you will see how he holds others dear who holds himself so cheap' (i.e. how much consideration you will get from the mercenaries, who have so little self-respect as to sell their services).

76-7 The poet is merely urging the rulers of Italy not to worship idolatrously the unfounded reputation enjoyed by the foreign troops.

78-80 He believes that if the barbarians from the north (*lassù*) get the better of the Italians, this is not a natural thing, but the fault of his compatriots.

100   **qui:** i.e. in this world; hence *la partita* is departure for the next.

102   **arrive:** 3rd pers. sing. pres. subjunctive; *quel dubbioso calle* is the road to eternity.

103   **questa valle:** this vale of tears, the earth.

109   **in qualche bella lode:** in some praiseworthy act.

113-18 The canzone must be careful of the way in which it expresses its message, since it must go among haughty people, whose wills, through bad habit, are inimical to truth.

22 (CXXIX)

Separated from Laura, Petrarch abandons himself to the
countryside and to the fluctuations of his emotions and
imagination. He deludes himself into believing that Laura is
present in a rock or a stream, but such illusions do not last. He
comes to feel that only his physical presence remains and that
his true being is with Laura in Provence.

2 **segnato calle:** 'beaten track'.

4 'If there is a stream or spring on a lonely hillside.' The
verb *siede* is to be understood from l. 5.

9 **lei** and **ella** both refer to *alma* (l. 6). He means that his
emotions are reflected in his face.

11 **in un esser:** 'in one condition'.

12 **uom di tal vita esperto:** i.e. one who has experience
of a lover's life.

18–19 **che sovente in gioco** etc.: 'which often turns to
pleasure the torment I bear on her account'.

20–2 'And I should be unwilling [*a pena vorrei*] to change
this bitter-sweet life of mine, because I say . . .'

25 **in questa:** *cosa, ora* or a similar word is to be understood: 'and so . . .'

30–2 **molle / de la pietate:** i.e. wet with the tears which
my self-pity provokes.

33–7 'But for as long as (*mentre*) I can hold my wandering
attention (*la mente vaga*) fixed (*fiso*—adv.) on my first thought

[i.e. of Laura] and contemplate her and forget myself, I feel love so close that my soul finds satisfaction in its own error.'

42   **veduto viva:** to be taken with *I' l' ho* (l. 40).

43   **sí fatta:** i.e. so beautiful.

44   **sua figlia:** i.e. Helen of Troy.

45   'like a star outshone by the sun'.

50   **pur lí medesmo:** 'in that very same spot'.
assido etc.: 'I sit down, a dead stone on living stone', cf. *Aen.*, I, 167: *vivoque sedilia saxo*: 'seats on living rock'.

53   because it is higher than all other mountains.

54   **piú espedito giogo:** 'least obstructed ridge'; cf. *Purg.*, xx, 4–5.

56   **i miei danni:** 'my losses', i.e. the distance between himself and Laura, but also the suffering which Laura causes him.

58   'my heart heavy with a cloud of pain': perhaps a reference to the theory that in times of stress the blood tended to concentrate at the heart.

62   *dico* is to be understood.

68   **un ruscel corrente:** presumably the Sorgue, which rises in Vaucluse.

23 (CXXXII)

The poet speculates on the contradictory aspects and. effects of his love for Laura; to these he gives compressed and vigorous expression by means of vivid antitheses.

5 **a mia voglia:** 'of my own free will': the poet is asking why, if he loves willingly, he should feel the need to weep and complain.

8 'how can you exercise so much power within me, if I do not consent to it?'

10–11 The poet pictures himself driven hither and thither by contrary winds (conflicting words and passions) as he sails the high seas (of love) in a fragile little craft (his own weak nature) which has lost its rudder (the control of reason). See also 30 (CLXXXIX) and 41 (CCLXXII), ll. 10–14.

24 (CXXXVI)

This is the first of three sonnets (CXXXVI–CXXXVIII) directed against the papal court at Avignon, where Clement V had transferred the papal residence in 1305. There, according to both Petrarch and Dante (see for example *Purg.*, XXXII, 149f.), the Church descended to depths of lust, simony, and depravity never before reached. Both poets desired as a first step in the reform of the Church that the papacy should return to Rome.

1 **su le tue treccie:** Petrarch has in mind the Great Whore of *Revelations* XVII, which both he and Dante (*Purg.*, XXXII, 149) interpreted as a symbol of the depraved Church.

2 **dal fiume e da le ghiande:** He symbolises in the river and the acorns the purity and simplicity of diet of the early

Christians, although the image of the acorns had been used by
Latin poets in their descriptions of the Golden Age (e.g.
Virgil, *Georg.*, 1, 148; Ovid, *Met.*, 1, 106).

3 **per l' altrui impoverir:** he refers to the rapaciousness
of the Church.

5 **nido di tradimenti:** cf. *Inf.*, xv, 78, where Dante calls
Florence *nido di malizia tanta*.

7 **de vin serva:** In his letters Petrarch says on several
occasions that one of the reasons why the cardinals were
opposed to a return to Rome was the quality of the wine of
Beaune.

8 **fa l' ultima prova:** 'reaches its extreme form'.

10 **trescando:** 'living a depraved life'.

11 **co' mantici:** i.e. to blow the fire of lust.
co li specchi: probably as an added refinement in their
sexual practices.

12 **in piume:** 'among feathers' i.e. in luxury.

25 (CLIX)

Petrarch wonders where in heaven Nature found the ideal
beauty of which Laura's face is the physical counterpart.
Certainly, on earth he can discover nothing that can stand
comparison with her loveliness.

1–4 Petrarch approaches Platonic doctrine in seeking an
idea of which the beauty he admires on earth is a physical
embodiment.

8 '. . . although the greatest of them [i.e. of the virtues mentioned in l. 7] is guilty of my death', a reference to Laura's chastity, which is the cause of the poet's despair.

14 cf. *dulce ridentem / Lalagen amabo, dulce loquentem* (Horace, *Odes*, I, xxii, 23–4): 'I shall love sweetly smiling and sweetly speaking Lalage.'

26 (CLX)

In all her actions Laura demonstrates more than human qualities.

4 **che:** either a relative pronoun or a causal conjunction.

6 **fide:** 'trustworthy' (unlike the stars of heaven which may deceive both sailors and astrologers).

11 **candido seno:** see note to 20 (CXXVI), 9.

12 **stagione acerba:** spring, or perhaps the youth of Laura.

14 **un cerchio:** a garland.
l'oro: her hair.

27 (CLXIV)

It is night, and there is peace over land and sea. But there is none for the poet: for Laura's image is always before him. Yet she is the source of both sweetness and bitterness, of comfort as well as of distress.

11 'one hand alone (i.e. Laura's) it is that both heals and wounds me'.

12 'And in order that my suffering should have no end . . .'
The description of night in this poem recalls passages from
both Virgil (*Aen.*, IV, 522–32) and Statius (*Silvae*, V, iv).

28 (CLXX)

In CLXIX he had stated that it was impossible for him even to
begin to tell Laura of his feelings: here he takes up the theme
again and concludes that inarticulateness is characteristic of all
who love deeply.

1 **dal bel sembiante umano:** i.e. when she shows a certain consideration for him in her expression.

2 'I have taken the bold decision (*ho preso ardir*) with my
trusty companions to assault . . .' The whole sentence is a
metaphor from war; but it is difficult to see what exactly *le mie
fide scorte* are: on the evidence of LXXV, 7–8 and CCLXXIV, 6 they
would be thoughts and emotions: but it is impossible to be
certain.

4 **piano:** 'modest'.

5 'Her eyes (when she looks at me) render my intention
vain'.

6–7 **ogni mia fortuna** etc.: objects of *ha posto* in l. 8.

8 **quei che solo il po far:** presumably love.

10 **altro che:** 'except'.

12 **caritate accesa:** i.e. pure but passionate love.

13 **altrui:** 'of men'.
gli spirti 'wits'.

29 (CLXXXIII)

If Petrarch suffers even when Laura looks upon him kindly, if she so affects him when she merely speaks or smiles, what will become of him if she turns against him? Experience shows that he is right to be disturbed at the prospect: woman is fickle.

3   'and if love gives her such power over me . . .'

5–7   '. . . alas, what will happen if, as a result of some fault of mine or of malignant fate, she banishes pity from her eyes . . . [lit. separates her eyes from pity]'.

9   **Però:** 'therefore'.

30 (CLXXXIX)

Petrarch allegorises his hopeless condition in the figure of a ship at the mercy of a storm.

Whatever may have been Petrarch's original intentions, it seems best, given the poem as it is, not to make more than the most general correlation between the various parts of the ship mentioned in the poem and particular aspects of Petrarch's psyche. Thus the oars (l. 5) may signify the will: the sail (l. 7) the sensitive soul: and the shrouds (l. 10) the dictates of reason: but not necessarily so, and it is best to allow these images their freedom as images.

1   **oblio:** presumably oblivion of his duties as man and Christian.

4   **'l signore:** i.e. passion, but not necessarily the passion of love.

5   The verb is *siede*, understood from l. 4.

7   **la vela:** object.

10   **rallenta:** 'slacken'.

12   **segni:** either *la ragion e l'arte* of l. 13 or the eyes of
Laura (cf. CLX, 6).

See also 23 (CXXXII), 10–11 and 41 (CCLXXII), 10–14.

3 1 (CXCII)

Petrarch calls upon love to join with him in contemplating
Laura's beauty: it is such that the grass and flowers beseech
her to tread on them and heaven rejoices in being made serene
by her eyes.

1   **la gloria nostra:** Laura.

5   **...dora e 'mperla e 'nostra:** 'adorns with gold and
pearls and purple'. What we believe to be so adorned will
depend on our interpretation of *abito* in the next line. This may
mean only what Laura is wearing. Some commentators, however, have taken it to refer to her person, in which case *dora e
'mperla e 'nostra* would refer to the colours of her hair, her
teeth and her cheeks.

8   'through this shaded cloistered place among the lovely
hills . . .' Vaucluse.

32 (CCVIII)

As he travels towards France Petrarch addresses the Rhone:
he asks the river to carry a message for him to Laura. She must
excuse his tardiness on the grounds of his exhaustion.

1 **Rapido fiume:** reference to the speed of the Rhone is
found in the *Apocolocyntosis*, attributed to Seneca, and in the
poem of Claudian against Rufinus. But then Petrarch had also
seen the river.

2 'wearing away the place from which you take your name':
a punning reference to the supposed origin of the name
Rhodanus, which according to Pliny (III, 4) was derived from
a defunct colony of Rhodes, called Rhoda.

7–8 **fiso u' si mostri attendi...:** 'look intently for
where is revealed the greenest grass and the serenest air.'

10 **la riva manca:** on the left bank were situated Avignon
and the residence of Laura.

13 **sie** = *sia.*

14 clearly based on *Mark*, XIV, 38: *Spiritus quidem promp-
tus, caro vero infirma.* 'The spirit truly is ready, but the flesh
is weak.'

33 (CCXIX)

Petrarch is awakened by the birds and the streams at dawn.
He recalls how he saw the sun make the stars disappear, only
to fade in turn when Laura came into view.

1 **cantar novo:** the birds' song, new every morning.

5 **Quella:** Aurora (or Eos), the goddess of dawn, loved

Tithonus, the son of Laomedon and brother of Priam, to whom
she remained faithful (hence l. 6). Although she begged Zeus
to make Tithonus immortal, she neglected to obtain eternal
youth for him, with the result that he became old and
shrivelled.

7   **amorosi balli:** the activities of the birds.

10   **seco:** 'with her'; **l' altro:** the other sun, i.e. Laura.

12   **gli:** *li* 'them'.

14   **quel:** the sun, i.e. Petrarch saw the sun make the stars
disappear and then saw Laura cause him (the sun) to fade.

34 (CCXXVI)

Separation from Laura means solitude and desolation day and
night, and the end of all pleasure.

1   **Passer mai solitario:** the image is from *Psalm* CII, 7:
'I watch and am as a sparrow alone upon the house top'.

9–10   That death is a relation or more specifically the
brother of sleep, is almost a commonplace in classical authors
(e.g. Virgil, *Aen.*, VI, 278: *consanguineus Leti Sopor*).

35 (CCXXXIV)

To the solitude of his own room and bed the poet once turned
for rest and for shelter from the storms of life. Now he cannot
bear to be alone with his thoughts and feelings and seeks refuge
in the vulgar herd.

6–7   **di che dogliose urne / ti bagna amor:** 'with what
urns of grievous tears does love bathe you'. Love is imagined

as being in the person of Laura, whose ivory-white hands, unjustly cruel to Petrarch, are responsible for pouring out the flood of tears.

11 **seguendol:** *seguendolo* 'while I followed it'.

levommi a volo = *mi levó a volo:* thought once raised him to noble heights.

12–13 Petrarch has previously shown a desire to avoid human company. Cf. 7 (xxxv), 3–4.

36 (CCXXXVIII)

An important nobleman, to celebrate whose visit a select group of ladies has been brought together, chooses from that group Laura, and honours her with a kiss: this act naturally makes Petrarch envious.

It is impossible to be certain of the identity of the man in question (assuming that Petrarch has a real person in mind): the most widely accepted thesis is that of De Sanctis, who put forward Charles of Luxembourg, son of John of Bohemia: Charles came to Avignon in 1346 to discuss with Pope Clement VI his election to the imperial throne: Petrarch, it has been suggested, saw in this meeting the possibility of a strong alliance between emperor and pope, and also of an eventual return to Rome by both authorities.

1–4 The nouns listed in the quatrain are without a verb. It is best to take them as a muted exclamation in praise of the visitor, rather than to resort to such artificial devices as understanding a verb or assuming that they are in apposition to *il buon giudicio intero* (l. 7).

1 **angelico intelletto:** i.e. which has reached the heights of moral and spiritual perfection normally reserved for the angels.

5   **sendo...eletto:** mod. *essendo stato eletto:* subject *un bel numero di donne.*

7   subject: *il buon giudicio intero.*

9–10 Construe: *comandò con mano le altre, maggior di tempo o di fortuna, trarsi in disparte.*

9   **maggior di tempo:** i.e. older, and for that reason worthy of respect.

o di fortuna: i.e. wealthier and also more nobly born, since birth too is a gift of fortune.

12   **con sembiante umano:** 'with a kindly expression'.

13   **basciolle:** mod. *le baciò.*

che rallegrò ciascuna: either because they saw in the honour paid to Laura a tribute to all of them or because they gladly recognised her superiority.

14   **strano:** 'uncommon': because of the fact that Laura was chosen from such a gathering and also because in Italy it was not customary to kiss women in public as an act of politeness or esteem.

37 (CCXLV)

An elderly friend, coming upon Petrarch and Laura, gave them each a rose, embraced them and told them that the sun never saw a finer pair of lovers.

3   **d' un amante antiquo e saggio:** of an elderly and wise lover, i.e. an elderly man wise in knowledge of love.

4   **duo minori:** Petrarch and Laura, who are younger than the donor.

egualmente diviso: one rose each.

11   This line presumably means that the gentleman stood between the lovers, placed an arm round each and looked now at one, now at the other.

volgeasi = *si volgeva*.

12   **Cosí partia le rose e le parole:** 'thus he shared his roses and his words'.

38 (CCL)

The image of Laura once consoled him in his dreams, but now it brings him warnings of her coming death.

1   **Solea:** subject *madonna* (l. 3): *lontana* agrees with it.

4   **aitarme:** mod. *aiutarmi* i.e. to help himself to escape from his pain and fear.

5   **parme:** mod. *mi pare*.

6   **pietà:** i.e. for Petrarch.

7   **fede acquista:** 'is convinced'.

8   **si disarme:** subjunctive: 'that it should strip itself . . .'

11   **sforzata dal tempo:** i.e. because it was late.

39 (CCLXIV)

Petrarch describes his conflicting thoughts and feelings: on the one hand, his desire for freedom from worldly interests; on the other, his appetite for fame and glory and his passion for Laura. Afraid, and conscious of his weakness, he must throw himself on God's mercy.

4   **ad altro lagrimar:** no longer tears caused by love, but tears occasioned by the approach of death and the poet's fears for his salvation.

5   **il fin:** death.

6   **quell' ale:** of divine grace.

11   **per ragion:** 'rightly, justly'.

14   **Quelle pietose braccia:** i.e. Christ's.

17   **altrui:** of those who postponed repentance until it was too late.

18   **altri:** wordly passions.

19   **L'un penser...:** In this stanza he expresses one of his conflicting thoughts: that he should free himself from attachment to the world and its pleasures.

21   **misera** is fem. because it refers to *mente* (l. 19).

30   **in lui:** in the false and transient pleasure which the deceitful world offers Man.

36   'and it is none too soon to start'.

38   **colei:** Laura.

39-40   'and I wish, for the sake of greater peace for myself (*nostra*), that she were yet to be born'.

43-4   **là dove forse...:** 'where perhaps no flame could enter lit by the torch of another woman'.

47   The day that Petrarch has awaited (he judges it to be

a good thing for his salvation that it has never come) is the day of Laura's yielding to him.

48 **or ti solleva** is imperative (the practice of pronominal enclisis up to the Quattrocento being different from that in modern usage).

51-4 'for if a movement of the eyes or a conversation or song calms your longing, which is so happy here on earth (*qua giù*) with what is harmful to it (*del mal suo...lieta*) how great will that [heavenly] pleasure be, if even this [earthly one] means so much to you?'

55 **un pensier dolce et agro:** this is the thought of glory. It is presumably *dolce et agro* because it is compounded of hope and fear.

63 **m'addormiva:** 1st pers. sing. imperfect indic.

68-9 But even if Latin and Greek (i.e. even if the most cultured people in the world) speak of Petrarch after his death, such fame will still be a vain thing (*vento*). Cf.

> Non è il mondan romore altro ch'un fiato
> di vento   (Dante, *Purg.*, xi, 100-1)

70-2 Since Petrarch fears that, in pursuing fame on earth, he has been accumulating only what an hour (i.e. that of death) will disperse, he wishes to embrace the truth.

73 **ma quell' altro voler:** his amorous passion.

74 **adugge:** 3rd pers. sing. pres. subj. of *aduggiare*. This means to cast a shadow over, as when a tree deprives the plants that grow beneath it of sunshine. (*Uggia*, 'deep shade'.)

75 **parte:** 'meanwhile'.

76 **non calme:** *non mi cale.*

80 **valme:** *mi vale.*

81 **spalme:** 3rd pers. pres. subj. of *spalmare* 'to tar [the hull]'. The poet asks what it avails him to have tarred the hull of his boat if it is held back among the rocks by two knots (love of glory and of Laura).

84 **dagli altri:** 'from the other [knots] . . .' i.e. other worldly desires.

89 **parme:** *mi pare.*

91-2 Cf. Ovid:

> Quid faciam video, nec me ignorantia veri
> Decipiet sed amor (*Met.*, VII, 92-3).

'I see what I do and it is not ignorance of the truth which will deceive me, but love.'

92-4 **mi sforza amore...:** 'love saps my strength, for he never allows anyone who trusts him too far to follow the path of honour'.

101 'is all the more improper in him who most seeks praise'.

102 **questo** refers to the *disdegno* of l. 96.

104 **perch' ell':** 'although (however much) she . . .'.

107 **quella:** Laura.

108 'for she was too pleasing to me and to herself' ('to herself' because she was proud).

109 **che spazio:** 'how much time'.

115 The poet sees himself grow white with age.

120-2 'I consider where I lost the right way, which leads to a safe haven . . .'

124-6 A certain earthly pleasure (love for Laura) is so deeply rooted in him that it does not leave him, but dares to bargain with death, i.e. will not abandon him until death itself takes him.

130 **subbio:** 'beam' (of a loom); the poet is telling us that the pattern of his life is already nearly completely woven.

136 Cf.   Video meliora, proboque,
      Deteriora sequor (Ovid, *Met.*, VII, 20-1).

'I see the better course and approve of it; I follow the worse.'

40 (CCLXVIII)

Laura died on April 6th, 1348, as Petrarch himself wrote in a note in his copy of Virgil. Here he speaks of her death and its consequences for himself, which are various and conflicting: on the one hand, he feels desolate because the physical Laura has been destroyed, and hence the world, which did not in the first place deserve the honour of such a being, has lost any grace it had; on the other hand, he realises that Laura has been perfected in paradise, and may assist him to his own salvation. But his despair is strong, and it is only the realisation that Laura wishes him well, and also desires that he continue to celebrate her, that prevents him from committing suicide.

For the thought and phrasing of much of the poem compare *Vita Nuova*, Chapters XXXI-III.

1 Cf. the lines of Q. Catulus given by Aulus Gellius (*Noctes Atticae*, XIX, 9.25):

    Ibimus quaesitum: verum, ne ipsi teneamur
      Formido. Quid ago? Da, Venus, consilium.

'We shall go to ask: but I am afraid that we may ourselves hold back. What shall I do? Venus, give advice.'

8 **di qua:** i.e. on earth.

12–13 'Love, you realise how harsh and heavy is the loss because of which (*ond'*) I complain to you.'

17 **n' è scurato:** 'is darkened for us'.

20 **orbo:** 'blind' because the world does not realise its loss.

33 i.e. it is only through weeping that he consoles himself at all.

35–6 **far del cielo / e del ben di lassú fede fra noi:** 'to be a testimony to us of heaven and the goodness above'.

38 **velo:** i.e. the body.

39 'which here was a shade [i.e. to her soul] in the flower of her life'.

40 **rivestirsen:** *rivestirsene*: She will put on the veil o her body again after the resurrection of the dead at the Last Judgement.

46–7 **come / là dove piú gradir sua vista sente:** 'as there where she feels the sight of herself to give most pleasure', i.e. as beautiful as she is in Paradise where her beauty is truly appreciated.

55 **al vero:** 'to the truth' i.e. to God.

59 **vincavi:** mod. *vi vinca*.

62 **tal:** *guerra* is understood; 'such a war that . . .'
altri: indefinite: he is deliberately vague as to whether he has God, nature, destiny or something else in mind.

65   **il nodo:** the knot that binds body and soul together.

68   **soverchie voglie:** 'excessive desires' (of a worldly kind).

70   **altrui:** 'to men'.

73f.   'And she prays that her fame, which still breathes (*spira*) in many places through your words, be not extinguished, but that you bring still brighter renown to her name.'

77   **né:** for *e* or *o*.

41 (CCLXXII)

He realises that life is slipping by, that death is approaching, and that there is no reason for satisfaction or even confidence in past, present or future.

The imagery of the sestet recalls no. 30 (CLXXXIX), and, as in the case of that poem, should not be given too rigidly allegorical an interpretation.

2   **a gran giornate:** a phrase taken from the terminology of travel: *una gran giornata* was a long day's travelling: to journey '*a gran giornate*' was therefore to travel quickly.

7–8   'Except for the fact that I have pity on myself, I should already be outside these thoughts', i.e. except for the fact that he is afraid of damning his immortal soul through the act of suicide, he would have put a stop to these reflections by killing himself.

9–10   'Any sweetness (*dolce*) that my sad heart ever felt returns to my mind's eye (*tornami avanti*)'.

12   **fortuna:** 'storm, disaster'.

13   The helmsman (*nocchier*) is probably reason: the mast

(*arbore*) and the shrouds (*sarte*) are presumably other qualities of the mind.

arbore: here fem. sing.

14 **i lumi bei:** on a literal level the stars: but they suggest also the eyes of Laura, cf. no. 26 (CLX), 7–8. **soglio:** 'I was accustomed'; the pres. was used with imperfect value. Cf. Dante, *Rime*, XCI, 6 (F & B, no. 68).

42 (CCLXXIX)

If Petrarch, meditating on love, hears the song of birds, the rustle of leaves in a summer breeze or the murmuring of streams, he sees or hears Laura. She comforts him: he must not weep because she is dead, for she has gone to eternal life.

1–4 The infinitive phrases depend on *s' ode* in l. 4.

5 **là 'v' io seggia d' amor pensoso:** 'wherever I sit meditating on love . . .'.

6 **lei che 'l ciel ne mostrò, terra n'asconde:** 'her [Laura], whom heaven showed to us [by sending her to earth] and earth now hides from us, I see and hear . . .'

13 **ne l' interno lume:** when she appeared to close her eyes (i.e. in death) she was in fact opening them to inner light.

43 (CCLXXX)

Petrarch has never been in any place which more clearly turned his mind to love, but Laura from heaven urges him to disdain the world and its pleasures.

1–2 'I have never been in any place where I could so clearly see what I wished to see, since the time when I could

no longer see it', i.e. from the time when Laura was taken
from him by death.

7 **Cipro**: Cyprus was sacred to Venus, who, according to
legend, landed at Paphos when she emerged from the sea.

9 **òra** = *aura*: breeze.

44 (CCLXXXVII)

Sennuccio del Bene, a minor poet and a friend to whom
Petrarch had addressed several of his poems, died in 1349.
Here Petrarch consoles himself for his friend's death with the
thought of his new freedom, knowledge and joy, and asks
him to speak to various other poets in paradise, and also to
Laura.

3 **preso** 'imprisoned'. Petrarch has in mind the doctrine
derived from Plato that the body is the prison of the soul.

5-6 Cf. Lucan, *Pharsalia*, IX, 12-13, of the soul of Pompey:
stellasque vagas miratus et astra / fixa polis: 'having wondered
at the wandering stars and the stars with fixed poles'.

6 **lor viaggio torto:** i.e. the oblique path of the zodiac.

9 **la terza spera:** i.e. the heaven of Venus.

10 For Guittone d'Arezzo and Cino da Pistoia, see the
Introduction.

11 **Franceschin:** Franceschino degli Albizzi, a friend and
relative of Petrarch's who died of the plague in 1348.

13 **e son fatt' una fera:** 'I have become a wild beast'. On

the evidence of CCCVI, 5-8, it would seem that Petrarch has in mind not so much the bestiality of the animal as its desire to avoid all social contact.

45 (CCLXXXIX)

Laura has returned to heaven. Petrarch now realises that she was right to resist his advances and thanks her for it. He permits himself a little self-congratulation on the final balance: he has brought glory to Laura, while she has led him to virtue.

3-4   Earlier than Petrarch would have wished, Laura has returned to her own land (heaven), after her pilgrimage on earth, and to the star (Venus) appropriate to her (*par = pari*).

8   **con una vista dolce e fella:** she looked upon the poet benignly or severely, as was appropriate to his conduct.

11   'made me, though I was burning with love, think of my salvation'.

13-4   One of them (Petrarch) used language, the other (Laura) her eyes; Petrarch won glory for Laura, and she was responsible for virtue in him.

46 (CCXCII)

Since death has destroyed Laura, he himself is confused, and his poetic talent exhausted: he should stop writing.

1   He had written three canzoni (LXXI–III) in particular on the eyes of Laura. See no. 14 in this anthology.

4   **singular:** i.e. separate and different.

8   **poca polvere:** complement of *son*.

11 **fortuna:** 'storm'.

disarmato: i.e. stripped of its equipment.

14 Cf. *Job*, xxx, 31: *Cithara mea versa est in luctum:* 'My harp also is turned to mourning.'

47 (CCCI)

Back in Vaucluse, Petrarch finds all its familiar features un-altered. But he has changed, and his grief is infinite. Laura is dead: he has come to look again on the places she has left.

1 **Valle:** Vaucluse.

2 **fiume:** the Sorgue.

9 **l' usate forme:** i.e. they are just as they were when Laura was alive.

12 **Quinci vedea 'l mio bene:** from this hill Petrarch had been able in the past to see Laura. *Vedea* is 1st pers. sing. imperf. indic.

13 **nuda:** i.e. her soul has gone to heaven, leaving on earth her body (the *bella spoglia* of l. 14).

48 (CCCII)

A vision of Laura in Paradise, in which she shows herself much more well disposed towards Petrarch than she had ever done on earth.

1 **Levommi:** mod. *mi levò*

in parte: 'to a place'.

3 **'l terzo cerchio:** the heaven of Venus, cf. no. 44 (CCLXXXVII), 9.

6 **se 'l desir non erra:** either 'if my desire does not err' (i.e. if her desire is not so intense as to lead her to believe what she wants, not what is reasonable) or 'if your desire does not err' (i.e. if he maintains the purity of his desire, and is not led to desire worldly things).

8 **inanzi sera:** i.e. immaturely.

9 'My joy cannot be comprehended by the human mind'.

10-11 **il mio bel velo** (i.e. her body which she will recover at the last judgement) is the second object of *aspetto: quel che* etc. is in apposition to it.

là giuso: i.e. on earth.

49 (CCCIV)

Petrarch tells us that in his youth he wrote poems complaining of love and of Laura, but in those days he was inexperienced in composition. Now Laura is dead: if she had lived and he continued his lover's plaints, he would, in his maturity, have made even the stones burst out crying.

13 **con stil canuto:** i.e. with more mature style.

Bembo discusses this sonnet in his *Prose della volgar lingua*, II, xvii (*Prose e rime*, ed. Dionisotti, 1960, pp. 166-8), quoting it as an example of the contribution to gravity of style made by the use of strong consonant clusters at the end of the first syllable of the words in rhyme-position (*vermi, arse, sparse, ermi*, etc.).

50 (CCCX)

The return of spring brings Petrarch no pleasure: he cannot turn his thoughts away from the dead Laura.

1 **Zefiro:** the mild wind which blows from the west in early spring.

3 This line is only loosely connected grammatically to the rest of the sentence. With a little straining it is possible to understand *Progne* and *Filomena* as objects of *rimena*, and *garrir* and *pianger* as final infinitives. '. . . and brings back Procne to her chatter and Philomela to her laments'.

In Graeco-Roman mythology, Procne was the wife of Tereus, king of Thrace: unfortunately, Tereus fell in love with her sister, Philomela, and having violated her, cut out her tongue and hid her away: but she managed to inform her sister, and Procne, in vengeance, served up to Tereus their son Itys as a meal. Tereus tried to kill the two sisters but was changed into a hoopoe: Philomela became a nightingale, and Procne a swallow.

6 **sua figlia:** most probably Venus, given the stress on love in ll. 7–8. It is possible that Petrarch has in mind the two planets, Jupiter and Venus, which in the spring are favourably positioned with respect to each other.

8 **si riconsiglia:** 'takes a fresh resolve'.

11 **chiavi:** i.e. of his heart. Laura has left his heart locked, closed to all manifestations of joy and love.

5 1 (CCCXI)

The nightingale sings in the night, perhaps lamenting the loss of its young or its mate. Petrarch is reminded of the death of Laura. His sad fate leads him to conclude that nothing on earth gives pleasure and lasts.

1–4   There is a reminiscence here of Virgil (*Georg.*, IV, 511–15):

> . . . qualis populea maerens philomela sub umbra
>   amissos queritur fetus, quos durus arator
>   observans nido implumis detraxit; at illa
>   flet noctem ramoque sedens miserabile carmen
>   integrat, et maestis late loca questibus implet.

('Just as the nightingale, sorrowing in the shade of a poplar, bewails the loss of its brood, which a harsh ploughman has noticed and dragged unfledged from the nest, and it weeps all night, perched on a branch, renewing its sad song and filling the region around with sad laments.')

4   **scorte**: 'expert', hence tuneful.

7–8   The poet admits that he has only himself to blame, for he did not think that Death could reign among goddesses (*in dee*).

9   'It is easy to deceive someone who persuades himself that he is safe'.

52 (CCCXV)

With the passing of youth, Petrarch and Laura were about to enter on a period of calm, considerate, reciprocal love, but death deprived Petrarch of such happiness.

2–3 **sentia** and **era giunto:** first person.

4 **al fin:** 'towards the end'.

5–7 **a prender securtade...de' suoi sospetti:** 'to be reassured about her suspicions' (i.e. with regard to his intentions).

7–8 **rivolgeva in gioco...:** 'her sweet honesty turned my bitter pains to pleasure'.

13 **feglisi a l' incontra:** 'put himself in its way' (i.e. of the happy state of l. 12); **feglisi:** *gli si fece.*

14 **a mezza via:** i.e. when he was half-way towards the enjoyment of the happy state.

come nemico armato: cf. *Proverbs*, XXIV, 34, of want, *quasi vir armatus:* 'like an armed man'.

53 (CCCXX)

Petrarch is again at Vaucluse and visits the places in which Laura was born and brought up. His meditation leads him to conclude that he has served a hard master: for love made him burn while Laura was alive and makes him weep now that she is dead.

2 **'l bel lume:** Laura.

7–11   The nest is cold. Laura is dead while Petrarch lives. This is the opposite of what he has desired: for he once hoped that she would visit his grave and that tears for him would flow from the beautiful eyes that once made him burn with love. (Remember the canzone *Chiare, fresche e dolci acque*, especially ll. 14–39.)

13–14   'for I burned with love for as long as I had my fire [Laura] before me. Now I weep over the scattered ashes.'

54 (CCCXLVI)

So lovely is Laura's spirit that the angels and the blessed were filled with wonder on her accession to glory. From heaven she inspires Petrarch to follow her.

1   **Li angeli eletti:** the angels who remained loyal while the fallen angels sided with Lucifer.

3   **passò:** i.e. when Laura passed from this life to the next.

4   **pietate:** 'reverence'.

6–8   **perch' abito sí adorno:** 'for so beautiful a [spiritual] form never passed from the sinful world (*mondo errante*) to this noble place [paradise] in all this time (*in tutta questa etate*)'. Of this last expression two interpretations are possible. The first is that it refers to the age in which Petrarch lived (i.e. 'in all this present age') and implies merely that Laura had no equal among her contemporaries or immediate predecessors. The second (and more likely) is that it refers to the whole period that has elapsed since the age of Adam. This explanation can be supported by reference to another sonnet (CCCLIV) in which Petrarch says of Laura that no spirit since the time of Adam has been equal to her:

> Forma par non fu mai dal dí ch'Adamo
> aperse li occhi in prima...

10 **si paragona:** this means that she is on an equal footing with the most perfect.

11 **parte:** 'meanwhile'.

55 (CCCLIII)

He addresses a small bird, which has perhaps lost its mate and is singing sadly at the end of an autumn day, and compares its condition to his own.

4 'and the day and the gay months behind you.' This line closely parallels l. 3: the day and the summer are over, the night and the winter are coming.

8 **partir:** 'to share'.
seco: 'with him' i.e. with Petrarch.

11 'a thing which (*di ch'*) death and heaven so begrudge me'.

14 **m' invita:** depends on l. 12.

56 (CCCLIX)

Laura appears to Petrarch in a dream and tries to console him. Why should he weep for her when she has gone to a better life? He replies that he weeps for himself, left in darkness. Laura urges him to follow her example and to realise how unimportant worldly things are. In answer to his question, she explains the significance of the palm and laurel which she bears, and tells him of her present state.

1   **soave mio fido conforto:** Laura. Dante had referred to Beatrice as his *conforto* (*Par.*, XVIII, 8).

5   **pièta:** 'confusion, emotional disturbance'.

10   **ciel empireo:** the Empyrean, the highest heaven.

18-19   'does it so displease you that I should have left this wretchedness . . .?'

27-30   'Why would God and Nature have put so much virtue into a youthful heart, if eternal salvation were not the predestined end of your good work?' Cf. Paul, *Romans*, VIII, 30: 'Moreover whom he did predestinate, them he also called: and whom he called, them he also justified: and whom he justified, them he also glorified'.

31   'O you who are of the company of the rare spirits . . .'

36   **al latte ed a la culla:** i.e. while he was still in his infancy.

37   **amorose tempre:** i.e. the lover's condition, his sufferings.

44   **cogliendo omai qualcun di questi rami:** Laura, in exhorting him to gather some of these branches (the laurel and the palm), is urging him to win glory through his work.

48   Petrarch's own pen does so much honour to one of them—the laurel. Of it he wrote in one of his sonnets:

> Arbor vittoriosa, triunfale,
> onor d'imperadori e di poeti (CCLXIII).

49-50   The palm signifies victory. Laura deserved it because, in spite of her youth, she conquered the temptations of
the world and was mistress of herself.

50-1   The laurel signifies triumph. This Laura merited
because of her chastity. Elsewhere Petrarch described her as
being in heaven,

> ove or triunfa, ornata de l'alloro
> che meritò la sua invitta onestate (cccxiii).

54   **lui:** refers to the *Signor* of l. 52: hence, God.

55   **seco:** 'with him'.

58   **Non errar con li sciocchi:** Laura, asked whether her
hair and eyes are those that captivated the poet, urges him not
to share the error of the foolish, who imagine that spirits still
have their bodies.

60   **spirito ignudo sono:** i.e. spirit without flesh.

61-6   What Petrarch seeks (her earthly body) has long been
mere dust. But God has permitted her to assume her mortal
form for this consolatory visit. She will have her body restored
to her once more at the Resurrection, when she will be more
beautiful than ever. And she will be all the more dear to
Petrarch, having been both severe and compassionate towards
him, safeguarding his salvation and hers.

69   **s' adira:** she is probably expressing anger again because
he is continuing to weep.

57 (CCCLX)

In the court of Reason, Petrarch accuses love of having
caused him great suffering and of having led him astray: but

love, defending himself, argues that he has brought countless benefits to Petrarch. When, however, love and Petrarch turn to Reason for judgement, she refuses to say which of them is right.

Much of the poem is paralleled in the argument about love between St. Augustine and Petrarch in Book III of the *Secretum*, although the roles are different: in the *Secretum* it is Petrarch who defends his love for Laura, whilst St. Augustine attacks him.

1 He refers to love.

2 **fatto citar:** 'having been summoned to appear'.

la reina: i.e. Reason.

5 Gold was considered the purest of metals, because it was refined rather than corrupted by fire (see Pliny, XXXIII, 19): so here Petrarch suggests that his troubles and sufferings test and refine his soul. This is an image traditional in the lyric.

8 **ragion:** 'justice'.

9 **il manco piede:** the left foot was associated with misfortune, error and crime.

10 **nel costui regno:** 'in his kingdom'.

13-15 Cf. Ovid, *Amores*, III, xi, 1: *Multa diuque tuli: vitiis patientia victa est.* 'I bore much and for long: patience was conquered by wrongs'.

18 **feste:** 'joys'.

21 **stringer:** 'embrace', i.e. describe completely.

22 **d' esto ingrato:** dependent on *querele* (l. 23).

25   'To how much bitterness has he accustomed my life . . .'

28-9   **era** / **disposto:** 'I was by nature inclined . . .'

33-4   **ho messo** / **egualmente in non cale:** 'I have equally neglected'.

36-7   'always sharpening my young desire [i.e. not diminishing with age] on the evil whetstone' [i.e. by giving him fresh, false hopes]. Cf. Horace, *Odes*, II, viii, 14:

> ferus et Cupido
> semper ardentes acuens sagittas
> cote cruenta.

'and savage Cupid always sharpening his burning arrows on a bloody whetstone'.

39   **a che:** a verb is to be understood: 'to what purpose [have served me] . . .'

41   i.e. his hair is turning grey; cf. no. 17 (CXXII), 5-6.

45   'who has turned my bitter life into a sweet habit', i.e. the bitterness of his life has through habit come to please him.

46f.   In his *Epistole Metrice*, I, vii, Petrarch lists the various countries which he says love drove him to visit (although in reality his reasons were probably much more mundane) among which he gives Italy, France, and the more northern Germanic countries. It is these latter which he would seem to have in mind here.

49   'and every devious path (*error*) that entangles travellers'.

52   i.e. wintry weather in the months of summer.

55   **un punto:** 'a moment'.

56 **giunto:** 'overtaken'.

65 The subject is love.

66 **squilla:** the bell of the watch.

67 **villa:** 'town'.

69 **legno vecchio:** object.
rose: past of *rodere*, 'ate away'.

75 **tu:** i.e. Reason.

77 **l' altra parte:** 'the other party', i.e. the accused, love.

79 **senza defetto:** 'without omission'.

80-1 **l' arte / da vender parolette:** i.e. that Petrarch had been a student of law. Petrarch had as a young man studied law at Montpellier (1316-20) and Bologna (1320-6, with interruptions), but had desisted because he found the legal profession corrupt.

84 **lamentarsi:** dependent on *si vergogne* (l. 82).
puro e netto: agreeing with *lui* (l. 86).

85 **desio:** presumably the desire for wealth and honour.

91f. The inspiration for these lines seems to have been Horace, *Odes*, II, iv, 2-8, where Horace notes the heroes who have been subject to love for inferior women, and cites as his first and third examples respectively the love of Achilles for the slave-girl Briseis, and the love of Agamemnon for the captured Cassandra.

91-4 All these nouns are objects of *lasciai cader* (l. 96).

91 **Atride:** Agamemnon, son of Atreus.

92 **Anibal:** Hannibal fell in love with a prostitute in Salapia, a town in Apulia. Petrarch presumably derived this information from Pliny, III, xi.

93–4 Order: *un altro il più chiaro di tutti e di vertute e di fortuna.*

94 **un altro:** probably Scipio Africanus Maior (see note to 10 (LIII), 37) who according to Valerius Maximus (VI, vii) loved a slave-girl.

99 **qual:** 'the like of whom'.
sotto la luna: i.e. in this world, under the lowest of the heavens, which was that of the moon.

100 **Lucrezia:** Lucretia, wife of L. Tarquinius Collatinus, was raped by Sextus, son of Tarquinius Superbus. Not wishing to live on dishonoured, she committed suicide. She became in literature a symbol of chastity and purity.

101 **idioma:** 'speech'.

107 **che di null' altra il tutto:** 'than the whole of any other woman'.

110 **avea:** first person.

113 **ferve:** literally 'boils', i.e. burns bright.

114 **conserve:** 'collections', both verbal and written.

117 **corti:** i.e. courts of law.

121 'and to tell in conclusion (*a l'estremo*) the great service [I have rendered him]'.

125 **schivo e vergognoso:** 'eschewing wrong and modest'.

126   **uom ligio:** the *om liges* of the Provençal poets.

127–8   'of her who left her noble imprint on his heart and
made him similar to herself'.

129   'what rare and noble qualities he has'.

134   **ne:** 'us'.
a Dio et a la gente: 'in the eyes of God and men'.

137–9   'I had given him wings to fly up to heaven via mortal
things, which are the ladder to the Creator, for the man who
judges well'. Petrarch here expresses a form of the Platonic
concept that sensible things may act as a ladder to the imper-
ceptible and ineffable truth. Cf. *Romans*, I, 20.

141   **speranza:** i.e. Laura.

143   **l' alta cagion prima:** i.e. God.

144   This concept appears for example in 14 (LXXII), 3, and
XIII, 10.

150   **chi per sé la volse:** i.e. God.

151   **al giusto seggio:** i.e. to the seat of Reason.

58 (CCCLXIV)

For twenty-one years Petrarch was ruled by his passion for
Laura; for another ten, since her death, he has mourned her.
Tired and fully admitting the error of his ways, he turns to
God and asks for release from this life and for salvation.

1–4   For twenty-one years (April 6th, 1327 to April 6th,
1348) love kept him burning, happy in its fire and full of hope

in his torment; it has kept him weeping for another ten since Laura and his heart went up together to heaven.

4   **saliro:** *salirono.*

7   **le mie parti estreme:** 'my last years on earth' (i.e. whatever time remains to him).

12   **carcer:** 'prison', the body.

13   **tramene...:** *trammene,* 'draw me from it safe from eternal pains'.

59 (CCCLXV)

Petrarch weeps as he thinks of the years he spent in loving what was mortal. He asks God to grant him His grace in order that his last days and his death may be worthier than his life.

3   **abbiend'io:** 'although I had'.

9–11   'So that, if I have lived in war and in tempest, I may die in peace and in port; and if my stay on earth was devoted to vanity, at least let my departure from it be honest.' Cf. Seneca, *Epist.*, XIX: *In fretu viximus, moriamur in portu:* 'we have lived on the high seas; let us die in port'.

12   **che m'avanza:** 'which remains to me'.

60 (CCCLXVI)

In this, the last poem of the *Canzoniere,* Petrarch addresses the Virgin, praising her and asking for her aid and intercession on his behalf, in order that he may finally renounce earthly love, rescue himself from a condition of sin, and die in peace.

The language and imagery of the poem are religious and biblical in nature, and in many ways the poem can be considered a reworking of such anthems of the Church as *Salve Regina* and *Ave maris stella*.

1-2 Cf. *Revelations*, XII, 1: *Signum magnum adparuit in coelo: mulier amicta sole et luna sub pedibus eius et in capite eius corona stellarum duodecim.* 'And there appeared a great wonder in heaven; a woman clothed with the sun, and the moon under her feet, and upon her head a crown of twelve stars.'

2 **al sommo Sole:** to God.

3 **sua luce:** Christ.

4 **amor:** both pure love of the Virgin and the earthly love he wishes to abandon. Cf. *Inf.*, II, 72, *amor mi mosse che mi fa parlare.*

5-6 **senza tu' aita / e di colui:** 'without your help and the help of him who . . .'

6 **colui:** the Holy Spirit.

7 **lei:** the Virgin rather than *aita* (l. 5). 'I invoke her who has always responded kindly to the man who called her with faith.'

9-11 'Virgin, if ever extreme wretchedness of human affairs brought you to show grace (*mercede*), consent to my plea.'

11 Cf. *Psalm* LXXXVII, 3: *Inclina aurem tuam ad precem meam.* 'Incline thine ear unto my cry.' (LXXXVIII, 2.)

12 **guerra:** the war between his conflicting impulses and emotions.

14–15 An allusion to the parable of the ten virgins (*Matthew* xxv, 1–13). One of the anthems in praise of the Virgin begins with the words: *Haec est virgo sapiens et una de numero prudentum.* 'This is a wise virgin and one of the number of the prudent.'

17 **scudo:** an image drawn possibly from II *Samuel*, xxII, 3.

23 **stampa:** 'imprint'. He refers to the wounds disfiguring Christ's body.

26 The relative pronoun (*che*) refers to *stato* but the real subject is of course himself.

28 A common concept in both hymns and religious literature, cf. *Par.* xxxIII, 1 and 6.

31 The same image occurs in a hymn attributed to Venantius Fortunatus: *O gloriosa domina...Coeli fenestra facta es.* 'O glorious lady . . . you have been made the window of heaven.'

32 **salvarne:** 'to save us'.

in su li estremi giorni: 'in the last days (of the world)'. According to Biblical writers (e.g. *Acts*, II, 17, *Hebrews*, I, 1–2) Christ was born in the last age of the world.

33 **soggiorni:** 'residences' i.e. the women who could have conceived and given birth to Christ.

35 Cf. *Luke*, I, 28: *Benedicta tu in mulieribus*: 'Blessed art thou among women.'

36 A common concept in devotional literature. (Cf. hymn attributed to Venantius Fortunatus cited above: *Quod Eva tristis abstulit / Tu reddis almo germine.* 'What sad Eve took away, you restore through the life-giving seed.')

40 **d' ogni grazia piena:** cf. *Luke*, I, 28, *Ave gratia plena*: 'Hail thou that art highly favoured.'

41 **altissima:** both 'most profound' and 'most exalted'. Cf. *Par.*, XXXIII, 2, *umile e alta più che creatura*.

43–4 So too St. Anselm (*Orationes*, L): *O tu, illa pie potens, et potenter pia Maria, de qua ortus est fons misericordiae.* 'O you, that devotedly powerful, and powerfully devoted Mary, from whom rose the fount of pity.'

49 Cf. *Psalm* CXXIV, 7: *laqueus contritus est et nos liberati sumus.* 'Our snare is broken and we are escaped.'

51 'In whose sacréd wounds I beg that you content my heart' i.e. that she bring him to peace in the wounded and forgiving Christ.

53 **senza esempio:** 'made on no model'.

53–55 cf. Sedulius, *Carmen Paschale*, II, 68–9. *Nec primam similem visa es, nec habere sequentem, / Sola sine exemplo placuisti femina Christo.* 'You have been seen to have no like either before or after you; alone of women, made on no model, you pleased Christ.'

55 Cf. CCCXLII, 5–6 (of Laura), *ma chi né prima simil né seconda / ebbe al suo tempo.*

56 These nouns are subjects of *fecero* (l. 58).

57   The Church fathers frequently refer to the Virgin as a
temple of God; equally common is the phrase 'fecund virginity'
of l. 58.

61   Cf. *Salve Regina*: *O clemens, o pia, o dulcis virgo Maria.*
'O clement, devoted, sweet virgin Mary.'

62   Cf. *Romans*, v, 20: *ubi autem abundavit delictum super-
abundavit gratia*, 'But where sin abounded, grace did much
more abound.'

63   In his *testamentum* Petrarch uses the same image: *flexis
animae genibus*, 'with the knees of the soul bent.'

67   The image is found in the hymn *Ave maris stella* and in
the Church fathers.

70   **senza governo:** 'without a helm', i.e. without the
directing power of reason.

71   **l'ultime strida:** the last cries of the drowning man.

73   **peccatrice:** refers to *anima* (l. 72).

75   Cf. *Psalm* XL, 12: *Non gaudebit inimicus meus super me*,
'mine enemy doth not triumph over me.' (XLI, 11.)

78   **virginal chiostro:** her virgin womb. Again a traditional image (e.g. the hymn attributed to Venantius Fortunatus mentioned above).

79-80   He refers to the tears, flattery and prayers he wasted
on Laura.

91   **sonsen:** modern *se ne sono.* **n' aspetta:** 'awaits us'.

92   **tale:** Laura.

93   **che:** picks up *tale* in the previous line.

95-7   'and even if she had known *(e per saperlo)*, yet that which happened would have happened: since any other desire on her part would have meant my death and the ruin of her reputation *(fama rea)*.' He means that if Laura had returned his love, this would have brought about the damnation of his soul, and the end of her good name.

100   'Virgin of high perceptions.' The blessed, and in particular the most blessed, are assumed to have senses which are far more penetrating and understanding than those of men on earth.

102   **altri:** Laura.

109   **sembianza:** 'image'. He has in mind the words of *Genesis* (I, 27): 'So God created man in his own image.'

111   **Medusa:** the Gorgon, whose eyes turned all who looked into them to stone, here symbolising the beauties of Laura. Cf. CLXXIX, 10-11; CXCVII, 5-6.

112   'dripping with vain moisture', i.e. his fruitless tears.

117   'as my first tears [i.e. for Laura] were not empty of madness'.

119   **del comune principio:** 'of our common beginning': presumably God rather than 'the humanity we share'.

120   cf. *Psalm* L, 19: *cor contritum et humiliatum, Deus, non despicies*, 'a broken and a contrite heart, O God, thou wilt not despise.' (LI, 17.)

129   **guado:** 'ford', i.e. the transition from this life to the next.

130   **prendi in grado:** 'accept graciously'.

137   **spirto ultimo:** 'last spirit', i.e. his spirit at the hour of death, as well as last breath.

SELECT VOCABULARY

Unless otherwise stated, nouns ending in -o are masculine, and those ending in -a are feminine. In cases where correct accentuation may prove difficult, the stressed syllable has been marked by an accent.

abbagliare, to dazzle
àbito, form; dress
accenso = acceso, alight, enflamed
accorare, to grieve
accordarsi, to be in agreement, harmony with
accòrgere, to notice
accorto, shrewd, wise
acerbo, bitter, unripe
acquetare, to calm, soothe
adagiarsi, to take one's ease, relax
adamantino, adamantine
adémpiere, to fill
adequare = adeguare, to equal
adirarsi, to become angry
adivèn = addiviene (*from* **addivenire,** to happen)
adombrare, to adumbrate, outline
adoprarsi, to act; work for, strive
ad ora ad ora, from time to time; continuously
adorno, beautiful
aduggiare, to overshadow
adunare, to gather
affannare, to trouble
affanno, anxiety, anguish
affaticarsi, to strain
affinare, to refine
affisarsi = affissarsi, to gaze on

affrenare, to restrain
affrettarsi, to hurry
agghiacciare, to freeze, turn to ice
aggia = abbia
aggradare, to please
agognare, agognarsi, to long for
agro, sharp, bitter
aguagliare, to equal, express adequately
aguzzare, to sharpen
aita = aiuto, help
aitare = aiutare
albergàre, to dwell
albergo, dwelling
allargare, to loosen; remove; widen, enlarge
allentare, to slacken
allontanare, to set at a distance, send away
alloro, laurel-tree; laurel
allumare, to illumine
alma = anima, soul
almo, divine; kindly
aloè, *m.*, aloe
alpestro, *adj.*, mountain
altamente, profoundly
altero, proud
alto, *adj.*, high; *adv.*, loftily
amaro, bitter
ambe, ambo, both
ammonire, to admonish
amo, lure
ancìdere = uccìdere

ancilla, slave-girl
anco = **anche**
animoso, noble-spirited
annidarsi, to find one's nest, make one's home
antivedere, to foresee
anzi, *prep.,* before; but rather
appagare, to content
appagarsi, to be satisfied
appannare, to tarnish, dull
apparecchiarsi, to prepare oneself
appiattarsi, to hide
appigliarsi, to follow, cling to
appressarsi, to approach
àquila, eagle
àrbore, *f.* = **àlbero,** mast
arco, bow
àrdere, to burn
arena, sand, earth
argento, silver
arme, *f. pl.,* tools; arms
arrestarsi, to halt
arrogare, to add to
ascóndere, to hide
aspro, harsh
assalire, to assail
assalto, assault, attack
assecurare = **assicurare,** to vouchsafe, protect
assecurarsi = **assicurarsi,** to feel secure
assènzio, absinthe, wormwood
assetato, thirsty
assìdere, to be seated, sit
a tergo, *adv.,* back
attèndere, to await
attorto, entwined
attraversare, to cross, pass between
attuffarsi, to plunge
augelletto, *dim.,* little bird
augello = **uccello,** bird
aura, air, breeze

aureo, golden
avanzare, to remain; proceed; exceed
avaro, greedy, grudging
avem = **abbiamo**
avere a sdegno, disdain
avestú = **tu avessi**
avrebben = **avrebbero**
avrìa = **avrebbe, avrei**
avvampare, to burn, blaze
avvèn = **avviene**
avvenire, to happen
avventuroso, fortunate
avvezzo, accustomed
avvolto, wrapped, surrounded

baldanza, boldness
basciare = **baciare,** to kiss
bavàrico, Bavarian
beato, happy, blessed
beatrice, *f. adj.,* blessing
beltade = **beltà,** beauty
biasmare = **biasimare,** to blame
bìgio, grey
bramare, to long for
bramoso, desirous
bue, *m.,* ox

c' = **che**
caduco, transient, frail
calare, to descend, sink
calere, to matter
calle, *m.,* pathway
calme = **mi cale**
cangiare = **cambiare,** to change
canuto, white-haired
capére, to be contained
càrcere, *m.,* prison
carco = **càrico,** laden
Caribdi, Charybdis
casto, chaste

cénere, dust; *pl.* ashes
cérchio, circle
cerviero, *adj.*, lynx-like
cervo, deer
cespo, bush
cétera = cétra, harp, lyre
cheggio = chiedo
chero = chiedo
chier = chiede
chinare, to lower; bow, bow down
chioma, hair
chiostra, enclosure
chiostro, cloister
ciancia, chatter, talk
ciglio, brow
cigno, swan
cima, summit
citare, to cite
cittadino, *adj.*, citizen
co = con
coce = cuoce
colle, *f.*, hill
colmo, full
colomba, dove
colonna, column, support
cóncio, reduced
confarsi, to befit, suit
conserva, collection
consigliare, to advise
consigliarsi, to resolve
contare, to count, to tell
contèndere, to contend
conto, known
contrada, region, country
contrastare, to oppose
contristare, to sadden
convèn = conviene
convenire, to be fitting, right, necessary
convertire, to convert, direct
core = cuore, heart
costoro, *dem. pron.*, those persons
costume, *m.*, habit

cotanto, *adv.*, so much; *adj.*, such, so great
cote, *f.*, whetstone
covare, to brood, hatch
coverto = coperto, covered
cre' = credo
crespo, curled
cristallo, *m.*, clear water
crudo, cruel
culla, cradle
cuòcere, *fig.*, to burn
curare, to care for, attend to

danno, damage, injury
da poi, afterwards
de = di
dei = devi
depigne = dipinge
depingere = dipingere, to paint
desio, desire, *m.*, desire
destare, to awaken
devea, deveva = doveva or **dovevo**
devoto, devoted, holy
devrìa = dovrebbe
dí, *m.*, day
die' = diedi or **diede**
dilettoso, delightful
dilivrare, to free, deliver
diluvio, deluge
dimandare, demandare = domandare
di pari, equally
dipartire, to take or send away
dirìa = direbbe
disacerbarsi, to become less bitter
disarmare, to strip, disarm
discovrire = scoprire, to reveal
disiare, to desire

disnore = disonore, dis-
honour
dispietato = spietato,
pitiless
dispregiatore, *m.*, scorner
disprezzo, scorn
distemprarsi = stemprarsi
disviare = sviare
dito, finger
diurno, *adj.*, daytime
divèllere, to uproot, eradicate
divulgare, to make famous,
make known
doglioso, suffering
dolce, *adj.*, sweet; *adv.*,
sweetly; *noun*, sweetness
dole = duole
dolersi, to complain
donde, whence, wherefore
donno, lord
dorare, to gild
dote, *f.*, gift
dramma, *m.*, dram, particle
dritto, *n.*, due, tribute
drizzare, to direct, place
erect
drizzarsi, to stand up
dubbioso, hesitant, doubtful;
fearful, dangerous
dumo, bramble
duolo = dolore

e' = egli or = i pl. def. art.
eburno = eburneo, ivory
ei = egli, he, it; they
elce, *f.*, holm-oak
émpiere = riempire, to fill
émpio, bad, evil
empìreo, empyrean
èrgere, to lift, raise
érmo, solitary
errore, *m.*, error, wandering
esaltare, to exalt

esca, tinder
esperto, experienced, proved
essèmpio = esempio,
example
estivo, *adj.*, summer
esto, *dem.*, this
estrànio = estràneo, alien
estremo, last
età, *f.*, age
etade = età
etate = età

face, (1) *f.*, torch
face (2) = fa
faggio, beech
fal = lo fa
fallace, fallacious
fallo, error
fantasma, *m.*, phantom, ghost
far riparo, to protect oneself
fasce, *f. pl.*, swaddling clothes
fascio, bundle, burden
fastidire, to vex
fattore, *m.*, maker
favilla, spark
fàvola, scandal; fable
fe' = fece
fea = faceva
fele = fiele, *m.*, bile
fello, severe
fera, wild beast
fermezza, stability
fermo, still, firm; sure
fero = fiero, cruel, fierce
fersi = si fecero
fèrvere, to boil; burn bright
fia = sarà
fiammeggiare, to flame
fianco, flank, body
fiata, time
fido, trustworthy
fìen = saranno
figura, manner; appearance
fioco, hoarse; faint

fiorito, flowery

fiso = fisso, fixed

flagrare, to flame, burn

foco = fuoco

folminato = fulminato,
struck by lightning, struck
down

folto, thick

for, fore = fuori

fora (1) = fuori

fora (2) = sarebbe

foran = sarebbero

forbito, polished

fortuna, fortune, storm,
disaster

fosco, dark, gloomy

fossa, grave

fostù = tu fosti (no. 24)

frale, frail

fraticello (dim. of frate),
friar

freno, bridle

fronde = fronda, leaf, leafy
branch

fronte, f., forehead

fuoco, fire

fur = furono

furare, to steal

gàbbia, cage, pen

gaio, gay

garrire, to chatter

gèlido, cold, icy

gelo, intense cold

gèmere, to groan

ghianda, acorn

ghirlanda, garland

giogo, yoke, ridge

gioire, to rejoice

giovare, to please; help

gire = andare, to go

giudicio, judgement

giùngere, to reach, catch

giuso = giú, down

gonna, clothing

governo, helm

gradire, to please

gravare, to weigh heavy

grave, wearisome, heavy

gravezza, weariness

gravoso, burdensome,
oppressive

grégggia = grégge, f., flock

grembo, lap

guado, ford

guaio, trouble

guardarsi da, to be on one's
guard against

guastare, to spoil

guisa, manner

i' = io

idioma, m., speech

ignudo = nudo, bare

imago, imàgine, f., image

imbrunire, to darken

impallidire, to turn pale

imperlare, to adorn with
pearls

impetrare, to obtain (by
asking)

importare, to signify

impoverire, to impoverish

impresa, deed, enterprise

inasprire, to render harsh

in bailìa di = in balìa di, at
the mercy of, in the power
of

incanto, incantation

inchinare, to descend; incline, bow down

inchinarsi, to stoop, bow

inchino, adj., bowed

incolpare, to blame

incontrare, to meet; happen

incostro = inchiostro, ink

incréscere, to displease

indarno, *adv.,* in vain
indi, from there, from then
in disparte, elsewhere
indurare, to harden
ineffàbile, ineffable
inerme, unarmed
infermo, weak, infirm
informare, to induce
infra = **fra,** among, within
ingegnarsi, to contrive
ingegno, mind
ingiuncare, to cover with rushes
ingombrare, to burden, obstruct
ingrato, ungrateful, unpleasing
in guisa di, in the form of
inondare, to flood
inonesto, shameful
intanto, meanwhile
intèndere, to understand, listen to
intenerire, to make tender, soften
intepidire, to grow tepid
interdire, to forbid
intero, flawless
intricare, to entangle
in ver', towards
inviarsi, to set out
invìdia, envy
ìnvolare, to steal
invòlvere, to enclose
iocondo, joyful
ire = **andare,** to go
iscolpire = **scolpire,** to sculpt
isfogare = **sfogare,** to vent
ìspido, bristling
ispirare, to inspire
ito = **andato**
iudìcio = **giudìzio,** judgement
ivi, there

làccio, snare
lacciuolo, snare
lagrimoso, tearful
lampeggiare, to flash, gleam
lance, *f.,* balance
lassare = **lasciare,** to leave, let
lasso, *adj.,* weary; *excl.* alas!
laudare = **lodare,** to praise
laureto, laurel-grove
lauro = **alloro,** laurel-tree, laurel
legare, to bind
leggiadretto, *dim. of* **leggiadro**
leggiadro, lovely; noble
lembo, edge, border
lentare, to lose intensity
letticciuolo, small bed
lezzo, stench
libertade = **libertà,** freedom
librare, to weigh; balance
lìcere, to be permitted
lido, shore; place
lieve, slight
lìgio, liege
limo, mud
lite, *f.,* law-suit
loco = **luogo,** place
lode, *f.,* praise; praiseworthy action
lontananza, remoteness
lume, *m.,* light; eyes, gaze
lupo, wolf
lusinga, adulation
lusingare, to deceive
lusinghiero, *m.,* flatterer, deceiver
lussùria, lewdness; lust

madonna, my lady
magione, *f.,* mansion
magnànimo, noble-spirited
magro, thin

maiestade = maestà, *f.*, majesty
maligno, malign
malo, bad
malvàgio, evil
manco (1), *adj.*, left
manco (2) **= meno,** less
mansueto, gentle
màntice, *m.*, bellows
marmo, marble
martìre, martìro = martì-rio, *m.*, suffering, martyr-dom
mastro = maestro, master
meco = con me, with me
mel = miele, *m.*, honey
membrare, to recall
menare, to lead
mentire, to lie
mentre, whilst, as long as
menzogna, *f.*, lie
mercé, *f.*, mercy
mèrito, reward
meschino, wretched
mìetere, to reap
minuto, *adj.*, minute
mirare, to look at, gaze upon; look for
miserere (Latin), *imp.*, have pity!
molle, *adj.*, wet
montare, to climb
mormoradore, *m.*, mutterer
moro = muoio, I die

navigante, *m.*, sailor
ne (1), *pron.*, of it, of him
ne (2), *pron.*, us, to us
nébbia, mist
neghittoso, listless
negro = nero, black
nembo, cloud
nemico, *m.*, enemy; *adj.*, hostile

nervo, sinew
netto, clean
'nfiora = infiora, *from* **infiorare,** to adorn with flowers
nido, nest, home
niegare = negare, to deny
ninfa, nymph
nocchiere, *m.*, helmsman
nodo, knot
noia, pain, suffering
nol = non lo
'nostra = inostra from **inostrare,** to adorn with purple
notturno, *adj.*, nightly
novella, news
novellamente, *adv.*, first
nube, *f.*, cloud
nudrire = nutrire, to nourish
nùvolo, cloud

obietto = oggetto, object
obliare, to forget
oblìo, oblivion
occìdere = uccìdere
occulto, hidden
odorifero, odoriferous, per-fumed
ogni ora, continuously
oltra = oltre, beyond
omai = ormai, by now
onde, from where, from what, wherefore
opera, opra, task, deed
óra, hour; *adv.*, now
òra = aura
orbo, blind
ordire, to plot
orma, footprint, trace
orso, bear
ove, if, where
ozioso, slothful

palude, *f.*, marsh
panni, *m. pl.*, clothing
paragonarsi, to be equal
parente, parent, relative
parmi, parme = mi pare
parte, *adv.*, meanwhile
partire, to depart; share
partita, departure
partito, plan
parto, parturition; child
pàscere, to feed, pasture
pàssero, sparrow
passo passo, step by step
pastorella, shepherdess
patteggiare, to negotiate
patto, term, condition
pauroso, fearful
paventare, to fear
pè = piede
pellegrino, *m.*, pilgrim
pellegrino, *adj.*, foreign; wandering
pelo, coat, hair
pena, suffering, pain
penna, feather, wing
pentérsi = pentirsi, to repent
perché (*with ind.*), because; (*with subj.*), although, in order that
percossa, blow
perdono, pardon
peregrinare, to go on pilgrimage; roam, wander
però, but; for that reason
però che, because
perseguire, to persecute
pesare, to weigh
pettinare, to comb
piacere, *m.* pleasure, beauty
piaga, wound, calamity
piàggia, slope
piagne = piange
piano, gentle, modest
pianta, foot

pìcciolo = pìccolo
piegare, to direct; bend
pièta, pietate = pietà
pietà, pity; reverence; confusion; suffering
pino, pine-tree
pio, compassionate; reverent
piuma, feather
po = può
poggiare, to climb, ascend
pòggio, hill, mount
pòi = puoi
polo, pole
pólvere, *f.*, dust
ponno = possono
ponsi = si pone
pòrgere, to hold out, proffer
poria = potrebbe
portamento, bearing
posa, rest, repose
pòscia, then
possendo = potendo
potéo = poté
prato, meadow
prègio, esteem, worth
prego, prayer
presso, *adv.*, near, close at hand
pria = prima
privo, lacking, deprived
procella, storm
prova, proof; experience
provvedere, to provide
pruina, hoar-frost
punto (1), point
punto (2), *p.p. of* **pùngere,** to pierce
pure, also; even; finally; yet; always
purgare, to purge

quai = quali
qual or, when, whenever
querela, complaint

questione, f., plea
quinci, from here

ràbbia, rage, fury
raddoppiare, to redouble
radice, f., root
rado, rare
ragionare, to reason, converse
rai, m. pl., rays
rallegrare, to make rejoice
rammentare, to remind
ramoscello, twig
rampogna, reproof
rappresentarsi, to present oneself
rasserenare, to soothe; clear
ratto, adv., swiftly
reale, royal, regal
recidere, to cut back
redurre = ridurre, to lead back; reduce
refrigèrio, cooling, relief
règgere, to direct; bear, support, hold up
reina, queen
relevare = rilevare, to avail
remo, oar
reo, guilty
reprèndere = riprèndere, to reprove
rèquie, rest
reservare = riservare, to keep
resùrgere = risórgere, to rise again
rete, f., net
retentire, to resound
rettore, m., ruler
rezzo, shade
rièdere, to return
rimanersi = rimanere, to remain

rimanse, rimansi = si rimane
rimanti, imp. of **rimanersi**
rimaso = rimasto, p.p. of **rimanere**
rimbombare, to re-echo
rimenare, to bring back
rincréscere, to cause regret
ringiovenire = ringiovanire, to rejuvenate
rinversare, to pour out
rio, wicked, pernicious
riporre, to preserve
riposarsi, to rest
riposto, secret, hidden
rischiarare, to brighten
rispóndere, to correspond, reply
ristorare, to restore
ritèn = ritiene
ritrarre, to portray; draw back
ritroso, uncivilised
riva, bank; end
rivo, river
roco, hoarse
ródere, to gnaw
romor = rumore, report
rosignuolo, nightingale
rozzo, unrefined, crude
ruina = rovina, destruction, collapse, decay
ruscello, stream

sacrare, to consecrate
saetta, arrow
saldare, to seal
saldo, strong
salma, f., burden
sanare, to cure, heal
sanguigno, bloody
sarìa = sarebbe
sarta, shroud
savere = sapere

sàzio, sated
sbandire, to banish
sbigottire, to dismay
scàbbia, scabies
scacciare, to chase away
scaltrire, to refine; sharpen
scalzo, without shoes
scampare, to rescue, save
scarso, weak; parsimonious
scémpio, torment
scerse, *past of* **scèrnere,** to perceive
schermire, to defend
schermo, protection, defence
scherno, derision
scherzare, to play
schiera, array, flock, class, host
schivo, averse
Scilla, Scylla
scoglio, rock
scolorarsi, scolorire, to lose colour
sconsigliato, devoid of counsel
sconsolato, disconsolate
scontrarsi, to encounter
scòrgere, to perceive; guide
scornarsi, to be dishonoured
scorso (*p.p. of* **scorrere**), fled
scorta, escort
scorto, expert; *p.p. of* **scòrgere**
scorza, bark; exterior
scurato, darkened
sdegno, disdain, anger
seco, with him
sècolo, world
securtade, *f.,* assurance
sèggia = **sieda,** *subj. of* **sedere**
sèggio (1), seat
sèggio (2) = **siedo**
segno, mark
seguitare, to follow

selce, *f.,* flint
selvaggio, wild
selvestro, *adj.,* woodland
sembiante, *m.,* appearance, face
sembianza, image, face
seme, *m.,* seed
sempiterno, sempiternal
sen = **se ne**
sendo = **essendo**
seno, bosom, fold
sensibile, sentient
sereno, *m.,* clear sky; *adj.,* clear, serene
serpe, *f.,* snake
serrare, to bolt, block, close
sfàce = **disfà,** destroys; undoes
sfavillante, sparkling
sferzare, to lash
sfidare, to threaten
sfogarsi, to give vent to one's emotions
sforzare, to force, do violence to
sfrenato, unbridled
sgombrare, to disperse, clear, dispel
sguardo, look
sie = **sia**
simigliare, to resemble
smalto, enamel
smorto, wan, deadly pale
snello, slender, agile
snodare, to loosen, untie
so' = **sono**
soave, sweet
soccorso, assistance
soggetto, *adj.,* subject; *noun,* subject; substance
soggiorno, resort; residence, habitat
solcare, to furrow
solere, to be accustomed
soma, burden

sommo, highest
sorte, *f.*, fortune
sospiro, sigh
sotterra, *adv.*, underground
sottrarre, to subtract, take away
sovèn = sovviene
sovente, *adj.*, often
sovèrchio, excessive, superfluous
sovra = sopra
sovvenirsi, to remember
spalmare, to tar
spàrgere, to sprinkle
sparso, scattered, divided
sparto = sparso
spelunca, cave
speme, spene, *f.*, hope
spera, sphere
spesso, *adj.*, frequent; *adv.*, often
spetrare, to release from stone
spigne = spinge, pushes
spirto = spìrito, spirit
spoglia, *f.*, spoglie, *f. pl.*, body, remains
sponda, edge
spronare, to spur
squadrare, to break in pieces, shatter
squilla, peal (of bells); blaring of trumpet
stagione, *f.*, season, time
stampa, imprint
stampare, to print
state = estate
stecco, stick, thorn
stellato, starry
stemprarsi, to lose one's powers, languish
sterpare, to uproot
stillare, to drip
stormo, *m.*, pack
strale, *m.*, dart

stràzio, torment
strido, cry
strìngere, to grasp, squeeze
sùbbio, beam (of loom)
superbo, proud
superno, *adj.*, supernal, heavenly
suso = su, *adv.*, above
sviare, to lead astray

tacere, to be silent, pass over in silence
tai = tali
talora, sometimes; perhaps
tardare, to delay
tardo, slow
tarlo, woodworm
tel = te lo
tela, web
temenza, fear
tempra, tempre, *f.*, tone; quality, temper
temprare, to temper
ten (1) = te ne
ten (2), tene = tiene
tènebra, shade, shadow
terso, clear
terza, *f.*, terce
teso (*p.p. of* tèndere), to stretch
tèssere, to weave
Tévero, Tiber
toccare, to touch; befall
tocco, *adj.*, touched
tomare, to fall
tormentoso, tormented
torto (1), *adj.*, twisted
torto (2), *m.*, wrong
tosco, poison
tosto, *adv.*, soon
traboccare, to overflow
tradimento, treachery
tradire, to betray
tragge = trae
tralùcere, to shine through

trapassare, to pass over, omit; to pass on to

trascórrere, to pass through

trasportare, to carry away

trastullarsi, to play

trattare, to discuss

travagliare, to labour

travagliato, wearied, worn

trecce, treccie, *f. pl.,* tresses

triègua = **trègua,** truce

trito, beaten, broken in pieces

troncone, *m.,* trunk

turbarsi, to be disturbed, troubled

u' = **ove**

udiènzia, hearing

umano, human, kindly

unqua, ever, never

unquanco, ever previously

usanza, custom, habit

usato, usual, accustomed

ùscio, opening, door

vaghezza, longing, restlessness

vago, wandering; charming

vaneggiare, to rave, act vainly

varco, opening, passage

vecchierello, old man

védovo, *adj.,* bereft

veggendo = **vedendo**

végghiare, to watch

véggia = **veda**

véggio = **vedo**

vela, sail

vello, fleece, lock (of hair)

vena, vein; rivulet

venale, venal

vene = **viene**

venir manco = **venir meno** to leave; fail, grow, weak

ventura, chance

verga, rod

vergare, to put lines upon, write

vergogna, shame

vergognarsi, to be ashamed

verme, *m.,* worm

verno = **inverno,** winter

vertú, *f.,* virtue; valour

vestigio, trace, track

vezzo, habit

vista = **viso,** face, appearance, sight

vivanda, food

vo = **vado**

vo' = **voglio**

voce, *f.,* voice, word

vole = **vuole**

voto = **vuoto,** empty

zappadore, *m.,* hoer, digger

INDEX OF FIRST LINES